MAESTROS & MONSTERS

MAESTROS & MONSTERS

Days & Nights with Susan Sontag & George Steiner

Robert Boyers

[M]

Mandel Vilar Press

Dryad Press

This book is typeset in Monotype Dante. The paper used in this book meets the
minimum requirements of ANSI/NISO Z39.48-1992 (R1997). ∞

Library of Congress Cataloging-in-Publication Data
Names: Boyers, Robert, author.
Title: Maestros & monsters : days & nights with Susan Sontag & George
    Steiner / Robert Boyers.
Other titles: Maestros and monsters
Description: Simsbury, Connecticut : Mandel Vilar Press ; Washington, DC
    : Dryad Press, [2023] | Includes bibliographical references and index.
Identifiers: LCCN 2023010977 (print) | LCCN 2023010978 (ebook) | ISBN
    9781942134886 (paperback ; alk. paper) | ISBN 9781942134879 (ebook)
Subjects: LCSH: Boyers, Robert--Friends and associates. | Sontag, Susan,
    1933-2004. | Steiner, George, 1929-2020. | Critics—United
    States—Biography. | Litterateurs—United States—Biography. | College
    teachers—United States—Biography. | LCGFT: Autobiographies.
Classification: LCC PN75.B64 A3 2023 (print) | LCC PN75.B64 (ebook) | DDC
    810/.9 [B]—dc23/eng/20230509
LC record available at https://lccn.loc.gov/2023010977
LC ebook record available at https://lccn.loc.gov/2023010978

Printed in the United States of America
23 24 25 26 27 28 29 30 31 / 9 8 7 6 5 4 3 2 1

MANDEL VILAR PRESS
Simsbury, Connecticut
www.americasforconservation.org | www.mvpublishers.org
and
DRYAD PRESS
Washington, DC
www.dryadpress.com

For Peg Boyers, always,
and for
Marc Woodworth & Emma Hanson,
beloved friends

CONTENTS

Part Two

Impossible to Tell: George Steiner

Part Three

MAESTROS & MONSTERS

15th Anniversary

Salmagundi

ART & INTELLECT
IN AMERICA

STEINER   SONTAG   LASCH
PAULSON   OZICK   FIEDLER
GARIS   KAUFFMANN   LUKACS
POPS   SPIEGEL   NACHMAN
MACDONALD   PACHTER   GRAFF
MUKHERJEE   MOLESWORTH   BOYERS

poems: Belitt, Warren, Nemerov, Peck,
Glück, Snodgrass, Kinzie, Wagoner, Flanner,
Dennis, Matthias, Eaton

two stories by J. L. Borges
Journal entries by R. Arnheim

reviews: Sedgwick, Lentricchia, Delbanco,
Fischer, Krupnick, Molesworth, Roth

A Quarterly of the Humanities & Social Sciences/No. 50-51, Fall 1980-Winter 1981
$4.00/ L 3.

Salmagundi covers for the
15th anniversary and
George Steiner memorial
issues.

Salmagundi Magazine

ART & THE PLAGUE DURING THE TIME OF CORONAVIRUS
TANCRÈDE HERTZOG

REMEMBERING GEORGE STEINER
MARTIN JAY • DAVID HERMAN • WILLIAM LOGAN

TRUMP: A SUMMING UP. AND AFTER?
AN EXCHANGE WITH TODD GITLIN & DAVID MIKICS

AFTER THE BEHEADING
FICTION BY STEVEN MILLHAUSER

JEFFREY MEYERS MANN & FREUD • JENNIFER DELTON TRADE IS NOT A 4-LETTER WORD
NEW WORK JOYCE CAROL OATES • ELIZABETH BENEDICT ON HONOR MOORE

FALL 2020 - WINTER 2021   NUMBER 208 - 209   £8 | $10

INTRODUCTION

*"[Walter Benjamin] defended the life of the mind to the end, as
righteously and inhumanly as he could."*

SUSAN SONTAG

*"'But I'm not one of them,' one wants to exclaim, displaying one's hands,
showing that one's hands are clean."*

J. M. COETZEE

"I don't think I ever wanted to be a great person after I knew Susan."

JAMAICA KINCAID

NOTHING is got for nothing."[1] So said Emerson, and
of course he was right. Go against the grain and
you are bound to pay a price. Piss off enough people by speaking what you take to be the truth and
you may wonder, now and then, why you bothered. Both
George Steiner and Susan Sontag earned the enmity more than
occasionally directed at them. That always seemed to me one
of their greatest virtues. They had no wish to be blandly accom-
modating, and assumed that their work would, frequently,
arouse misgiving, hostility, rebuke. They did not aspire to the
warm bath of social or cultural affirmation.

Of course, enmity that is an expression of a relentless, ill-
informed antipathy will hardly seem instructive or chastening,
even to those long accustomed to attack or derision. Far better
the opposition of those with some genuine stake in a quarrel.

To be opposed as a serious troublemaker is to receive an enormous tribute. To be vilified for negativism, or changing your mind, or refusing to state the obvious, or entertaining immoderate ambition is to feel that you have done what you could to invite the enmity. Did George invite enmity? Often yes, frequently no. In the 1970s the English scholar John Carroll suggested that the derision directed at Steiner had much to do with weaknesses noted by academics who wondered at his enormous ambition and influence. "Steiner's work is superficial, some say unscholarly," Carroll wrote. "There is a brilliant gloss, but essentially the analysis never penetrates deeper than journalistic sketchiness. Steiner's popularity among students merely illustrates the ease with which modern youth can be led away from serious, systematic criticism. Within the university he is a corrupting force."[2]

This sort of criticism was poisonous, an expression of a *ressentiment* George wondered at, and yet understood. In England he was resented for pointing out the monolingual provincialism of English literary culture, and for a variety of other indiscretions, including what another scholar cited as his penchant for writing "in an aggressive and haughty manner."[3] The term "journalistic," as applied to Steiner's work, was often an expression of envy felt by academics who couldn't quite accept that someone could write essays on challenging, if not arcane, subjects and reach a large, general readership in the best weeklies and monthlies. Likewise, the demand for "systematic criticism" signaled a preference for the kind of writing expected of academics trained in the protocols of the university. The notion that Steiner's work is marked by "sketchiness" can only seem absurd to anyone who reads his essays on Shakespeare, or Homer, or Dante, or George Lukacs, or his scholarly books on translation and the history of "Antigones." Steiner was, to be sure, provocative, and he often courted fierce opposition. But much of the enmity directed at him had principally to do with that "ill-informed antipathy" he neither deserved nor invited.

The hostility directed at Sontag could be comparably fierce, and she did, more than occasionally, bring it on. As with Steiner, she was often felt to be haughty and obnoxious. Her critical pronouncements could be categorical. Like Steiner, she sometimes worked "outward from the particular literary instance to the far reaches of moral and political argument," as George himself put it,[4] and thereby seemed to her critics to overreach. The tenor of the derision she attracted was especially notable in the attacks published in the *Nation* in 1982, a few weeks after she delivered at New York's Town Hall (on April 6) a blistering indictment of the American left, at a meeting convened to express what she called "our solidarity with the people of Poland, now languishing under the brutal oppression" of the Communist Jaruzelski regime.[5] Unlike other writers who asserted their opposition to "the utter villainy of the Communist system," Sontag delivered a mea culpa that was as well a nostra culpa, charging herself and her colleagues and friends on the progressive left with a failure over decades to acknowledge the sins of the Communist system for fear of seeming to join forces with the political right.

When Sontag asked, "Why did we not have a place for, ears for" the truths spoken by dissident anti-Communist intellectuals like the Czeslaw Miłosz who wrote *The Captive Mind* in 1953, she was derided by a host of intellectuals. Philip Green, a member of the *Nation*'s editorial board, denied the charges Sontag directed at the left, and characterized what she said as only "superficially plausible" and "in the end . . . ridiculous."[6] Daniel Singer, author of *The Road to Gdansk*, mocked her as a "converted sinner" and associated her with earlier intellectuals who argued "in equally primitive fashion."[7] The historian David Hollinger tried, he said, unsuccessfully, "to take Susan Sontag seriously," contending that "the genre of mea culpa into which Sontag's speech falls had been laughed out of existence years ago by Harold Rosenberg's 1955 essay, 'Couch Liberalism and the Guilty Past.'"[8] Wanting to thank Sontag for inviting "the left to criticize its own record," Christopher Hitchens, a contributing editor of the *Nation*, criticized her "ill-tempered and ahistorical remarks."[9] Such criticism of Sontag persisted over the decades that followed, even among those who were sometimes moved by the brilliance of particular books and essays she wrote.

Though both George and Susan often felt the sting of rebuke, and did what they could to provoke it, they never quite settled into the role of beloved dissidents or contrarians. Not for either of them the status of what Jenny Diski, in the *London Review of Books*, called the "dedicated social trouble-makers who . . . as the decades roll by," find that those they "wish to irritate" get used to them and even begin "to regard [them] with a certain affection." Not for either of them the status of "a beloved puppy that is always forgiven for soiling the carpet." Neither quite became a "licensed controversialist" at whom "people just smile and shake their heads."[10]

The contempt directed at my two difficult friends was often a function of envy. They were provocative writers whose essays and books created a constant stir. Sontag was certainly the most visible intellectual in the English-speaking world from the mid-sixties until her death in 2004, and Steiner was for thirty years a regular book critic for the *New Yorker* and a figure around whom international conferences were mounted—in Paris, Bologna, Madrid, Berlin, and other cities. Additional acclaim arose from the major awards, prestigious lecture series, honorary degrees, book sales far beyond what other critics and thinkers could imagine, even—in Steiner's case—frequent appearances on European television talk shows, seated across from the best minds and artists of his generation. How not to envy that sort of good fortune and to suspect that there was something unseemly about it? How not to feel that both gave off airs of unbecoming omniscience and self-confidence, as if they had taken to heart the words of Elias Canetti who in 1936 wrote, "I cannot become modest; too many things burn in me."[11]

I knew George Steiner and Susan Sontag for most of my adult life, George for more than fifty years, Susan for forty. Our intimacy, such as it was, had much to do with the fact that I founded the quarterly *Salmagundi* in 1965 and developed ways to keep both of them invested in the projects and programs I was sponsoring through the magazine and the New York State Summer Writers Institute. *Salmagundi* has always been a "little magazine." The term itself suggests modesty of scale and audience, but does not suggest the range of a publication that can take on—often in a sustained way—just about any subject, from kitsch and the new puritanism to the clash of civilizations and the consciousness industry. To run such a magazine for more than a half century, as I have done, is to be alert to prospects that are simply not plausible for trade publications, with their eyes fixed always on a large popular audience. Though Susan and George had regular access to the pages of large national magazines, including the *New Yorker*, they felt a peculiar affinity for a magazine that had its own voice and never pretended to be anything but itself.

More than a half century ago, Lionel Trilling wrote that the little magazine, at its best, aims to prevent "our culture from being cautious and settled, or merely sociological, or merely pious,"[12] and that seemed to me, as also to George and Susan, an apt description of what our little magazine set out to do with each issue. They felt that we were good at making "the official representatives of literature"—not to mention mainstream journalists and academics—"a little uneasy," doing what we could to "keep a countercurrent moving." We remained alert to the fact that most little magazines showed little interest in ideas, and often excluded from their pages anything resembling political content or debate. The major reason George and Susan were attracted to *Salmagundi* was its commitment to dialogue and contention, its willingness to invite as contributors people notable for changing their mind or for going against the grain of the "enlightened" consensus. Both approved what Christopher Lasch wrote in his 1975 "Introduction" to the tenth anniversary issue of the magazine:

> [*Salmagundi*] has often criticized leftist clichés . . .
> from a point of view sympathetic to the underlying
> objectives of the left. . . . [W]hen the "counterculture"
> hardened into a dogma of its own and the writings of
> [that movement] began to be treated as revealed truth,
> *Salmagundi* became increasingly critical of the new left
> or at least of its cultural manifestations.[13]

Though George was never a man of the left, he found in our pages and in our conferences an opening to engage with public intellectuals on the left—Edward Said, Slavoj Zizek, Jonathan Schell, Jackson Lears, David Bromwich, Christopher Lasch, and of course, Susan Sontag among them—in forums he would not have considered without our prompts and invitations. Steiner and Sontag were as committed as we were to challenging the notion, so deeply entrenched in our own left-liberal cohort, that good people like us were always in the right.

Critically important for my relations with George and Susan were the three-day conferences we ran almost every year on the Skidmore College campus or at The New School in Manhattan, and the special issues of *Salmagundi* that featured edited transcripts of those meetings. George and Susan delivered an assortment of prepared remarks and papers at a number of those meetings, and in reading the published transcripts—with contributions by such writers as Orlando Patterson, Martha Nussbaum, Kwame Anthony Appiah, Christopher Hitchens, Marilynne Robinson, Carolyn Forché, Bernard-Henri Levy, Breyten Breitenbach, and others—George and Susan had the sense that we were doing something no other magazine could do. Whether the subject debated was "art and ethics," "the triumph of the therapeutic" or "the future of black America," the spirited contention of *Salmagundi* conferences seemed to them infectious. My friendships with them were driven by our mutual attraction to cultural and political issues central to the life of the magazine. Did George often berate me for not attracting a readership beyond the usual size for a little magazine? He did. Did Susan not mainly send her essays to the larger circulation magazines like the *New York Review*? She did. And yet both counted themselves as members of our magazine "family," in what looked to others like a distinguished coterie. Both believed, with Trilling, "the word coterie should not frighten us too much."[14]

Hard to think of George and Susan as coterie writers when each commanded a large and diverse following. But then, in *Salmagundi* it was possible for them to take on issues impossible elsewhere—in George's case, for example, to launch an attack on American culture and have it answered, at length, by Sontag and a dozen other leading intellectuals; in Susan's case, to debate, over three days in 2001, the culture of museums, and thereby to test ideas and impressions with the American art critic Arthur Danto and with cultural theorists like Rochelle Gurstein and Philip Fisher, among others.

In a 1965 letter responding to the first issue of *Salmagundi*, the critic Robert Alter wrote that there is "little threat of the stifling coterie quality one feels in so many of our intellectual publications." No evidence, he noted, of an official political line. When Susan offered us a sentence to use in advertisements, she wrote simply that "*Salmagundi* is my favorite little magazine." She explained years later at a New York State Summer Writers Institute panel on magazine publishing that *Salmagundi* was "amiably plural," "unsystematic," and "never blandly virtuous."

As I go back over the preceding paragraphs, it occurs to me that they may be read *as an effort to unravel a mystery.* Why is it that writers who have no worldly or practical need to be associated with a little magazine, who have access to audiences far beyond what *Salmagundi* and its conferences can provide, should nonetheless agree to regularly invest themselves in its projects? I am tempted to say for "the romance of the little magazine" to describe an attraction that for some decades has felt "real." Certainly, the romance was real for George and Susan and for many others who became our friends and regular contributors. An example: One morning I had a phone call from Nadine Gordimer's agent, who reported what Gordimer had already told me at a New York City dinner a week or two earlier: she had completed a number of short stories that were ready to be sent out, but she wanted me to select what I wanted for *Salmagundi* before the agent sent the remaining fiction to magazines like the *New Yorker* and *Harpers*, which would pay her well. Wasn't that strange, the agent asked me? To which I could only say that, though Gordimer and I saw one another infrequently, we had become friends. Apart from my having written essays and reviews about her work, she was moved by the very smallness of our enterprise and the fact that for my wife, Peg, and me, *Salmagundi* was clearly a labor of love. The romance of it.

Another such exchange took place in Manhattan in 1987, when Peg and I were at a dinner to celebrate the awarding of the Bennett Prize to Gordimer. We were seated on either side of *New York Review of Books* editor Robert Silvers at a table for six. All very convivial. At one point, when Bob Silvers and the Boyers discovered that we had much gossip to share and laugh about, Silvers turned suddenly serious and said there was something he had to ask.

"It is striking, is it not, that Christopher Lasch, long a regular contributor to the *New York Review,* is now regularly sending new work to *Salmagundi,* while telling me that 'perhaps' he will later have something new to send me? Do you regard that as very peculiar?" Silvers asked.

"I do", I assured him, "and I find it hard to imagine that if you were asking me to write for the *New York Review* I would put you off."

"But then how do you account for it," he persisted. "I mean," he smiled, "what can you do for Kit that we can't?"

"Well," Peg said, "we can provide the sense that we need him and others like him, that there's something strange and maybe even noble about a little magazine that has an intense and devout following but none of the worldly power of a magazine with a hundred thousand or more subscribers."

NEITHER George nor Susan was always easy to be close to. In a 1980 essay on Roland Barthes—one of Sontag's heroes—she wrote that "his interest in you tended to be your interest in him," so that when he greeted her with the words "Ah, Susan. Toujours fidèle," she could feel that those words were apt.[15] She was always faithful. Always interested in him. George and Susan knew that I was faithful to them in that sense, wanting to know everything about what they were writing and doing and thinking. Still, neither ever quite suggested that I existed only to admire them and show them to themselves as they wished to be reflected. Both indulged me, allowed me to resist them, to argue with them—even in books and essays I was writing. If neither was in the least ordinary, "regular," companionably relaxed, they were, as the Cole Porter song has it, "always true to you, darling," in their fashion.

Strange that the enmity they aroused was in evidence even at the time of their deaths, the distaste obvious even in one or another obituary notice or send-up. George was never entirely forgiven by some for the theatricality of his pronouncements, the want of sobriety, the breadth of his reach. To her detractors, Susan seemed almost comical in the extremity of her ardor and the presumption of authority that informed her writing. "Romantic sentimentality" was one expression used to deride her, "showmanly" a term of derision directed at Steiner. Both were said to indulge in what G. K. Chesterton called "the base idolatry" of believing in themselves. Their enthusiasts were sometimes described as dazzled, awe-struck, and thus not properly disposed to resist them.

Both George and Susan were emblems of the NOT-ME. I was somewhat less avid, less provocative, less relentless, and it occurred to me that my own more modest nature was, for each of them, an attraction. Now and then I feared that they must think me bland, that my resolute commitment to a kind of sanity would seem to them a species of spiritual impoverishment. Others were fearful lest they be consumed in the company of two such imposing figures, thinking perhaps of the caution voiced by Jean Amery, who enjoined us to "be careful or you will burn, all ablaze, all a blaze."[16] But I was tempted by the heat, and the illumination, given off by my improbable friends, and they were apparently eager for my company, though I had reason to wonder how far the loyalty of such ferocious, even fanatic, persons might extend. I understood that George and Susan thought me weirdly equable, balanced, less than thrilling, however much I passed for electric and dangerous in precincts of the American academy.

Once, at the 2001 *Salmagundi* conference on the culture of museums, Susan told us that she was "very much an addict of engulfing experiences."[17] What exactly did she mean?

That when she went to the movies, she sat "in the third-row center . . . too close for most people." She did *really* want to be "engulfed." She wished to be "as little distracted by the presence of other people in the audience as possible." Just so for Susan at live performances of dance or music. The same for her in museums or galleries, determined not to be pressured by others to move along too quickly past works she hoped to study. A matter, Susan said, of "temperament," of liking "to be in the most intense contact with what I'm looking at, or listening to."

George, too, was an addictive personality—he also wished to be engulfed, ravished by works of art, undone by the reflections of thinkers he admired. He too had little patience for distraction. As with Susan his characteristic accent was high intensity. Though he did occasionally permit himself a leisurely chess match with a friend or a half hour in front of the television watching the evening news, he did not wish to relax. For George and Susan there was the drive to register the gap between worthy and unworthy pleasures, between trivial and demanding encounters.

Addictive, obsessive people are bound to be—at least some of the time—hard to take. Often with such people there is at least a grain of madness. When they are hooked on some idea, or on some*one*, they can tolerate no interference or diminution of intensity. George spoke often of his own susceptibility to an "autistic ecstasy . . . stronger than love or hatred." He meant it when he said that he couldn't read a newspaper without a pen in hand to correct errors. Like Susan, he could worship artworks that seemed to him immeasurable or incomparable. Both promoted what the British psychologist and essayist Adam Phillips called "a culture of close reading and slow looking, in which the arts are taken to be formative." Each believed that there was "catastrophe" in people "being too interested in the wrong things."[18] They refused to disguise themselves as impartial and had no use for provincial gentility. Both made being an intellectual attractive, however forbidding each of them could seem, however daunting the prospect of measuring up to their example.

In spite of their differences, George and Susan were as one in their attitude to the charge of elitism. I never knew quite how to defend them against that accusation. George was always ready to declare he had a calling which he would never negotiate. His pursuits were "infinitely self-rewarding," beyond justification, "a leprosy of obsession" which impelled him towards "a supreme effort." Would others applaud or approve that effort, that obsession? To think that likely was perhaps not fully to understand it. You did "that sort of work," George insisted, simply because "you have been chosen" to do it. His métier was "a vocation," answering "a summons." The sense that you can't "belong to our clerisy" without having answered that summons was powerful in George. Like Susan, he admired Elias Canetti as a "virtuoso of intransigence."[19]

Surprisingly, perhaps, the charge of "elitism" was directed as often at Susan, and though at first it seemed to her ridiculous, she came more and more to invite and even to welcome it. Early in her career she had been admired as the embodiment of the hunger to be in touch with everything new and difficult, high and low, popular and esoteric. In the sixties, she championed what she called "the new sensibility" in part because it was "defiantly pluralistic," and yet she saw herself as "a newly minted warrior in a very old battle against philistinism," against "frivolity" and "shallowness." In "Notes on 'Camp,'" the essay that brought her fame, she acknowledged that "I am strongly drawn to Camp, and almost as strongly offended by it."[20] Hers was "a deep sympathy modified by revulsion." Those who took her to be of one mind, at one with the brazen, the coarse, the countercultural, the merely playful or transgressive, did not read her carefully, and as she developed they were disappointed by her betrayal of a unitary posture she had never adopted. Like Steiner, she was never reluctant to characterize what she disliked as "banal," "coarse," "mid-cult," "kitsch," or "philistine." Neither of them was a spokesperson for the *zeitgeist*, for the dominant attitudes of the cultural moment.

George spoke often of "the scandal of American secondary schooling" and of the "dilemma of the relation between democracy and excellence." Nonetheless, he was aware that his alienation from most things American made him a dubious critic of the culture. "It is my fault," he wrote in a letter of January 1992, "that I am drifting out of contact with America, at the very time when the children [David Steiner and Deborah

Steiner] are planting roots there. . . . But I so hate political correctness, the litigation-madness of daily American existence, the sub-literacy, the violence and cult of violence, the utter mediocrity of what passes for political leadership . . . that I find myself getting reflexes wrong, and over-simplifying." Though I was hardly an ideal source of information about all things American, I was always honest with George when I thought he had exaggerated or oversimplified, and he assured me in that same letter, "I need and want your objections. Your letters are 'inner punctuation marks' as I try to hammer things out." The ever-present gaps in our sense of things in no way compromised our relation. When he wrote in October 1975 that "you will recognize the healthy stringency of our relation if I say that I am a bit let down" by a particular special issue (on liars and lying) of *Salmagundi* magazine, I understood that our efforts to understand American society with ideas informed by psychoanalytic critics like Norman O. Brown and Robert Jay Lifton would not seem to him especially helpful. "I really attach far less interest than you do to psychoanalysis," George wrote, "and the whole confessional-therapeutic circus." But then we differed on other questions, including his low estimation of many American artists and writers I admired. Regarding the "dilemma of the relation between democracy and excellence," I was always reluctant to make categorical judgments, and told him so. When—for an anthology devoted to considerations of his work—I disputed aspects of the case he made in his notorious "Archives of Eden" essay, he was grateful "for the correction" and not at all defensive.[21]

Susan's criticism of American culture and what she took to be its effects on contemporary institutions was often as harsh and categorical as anything to be found in George's works. At the 2001 *Salmagundi* conference on "An Age of Museums,"

Susan lamented "the disgraceful demotion of some of the greatest paintings at the Musée D'Orsay to a cramped, low-ceiling space near the cafeteria upstairs." She also noted "the radical relativism that has prevailed in the name of bringing art closer to life in a democratic society." Here, she continued, "is nothing less than the destruction of what is special, or transfig-uring, or nourishing about the experience of art." As in other efforts to work through her own ambivalences about art and democracy, Susan was never less than forthright, occasionally brutal, as in exchanges with the museum director David Ross at the "Museums" conference. Content to speak as a lover of museums and of those entrusted with their care, she could not but note the growing tendency, in cultures like ours, "to con-sider whatever has been around for a long time as 'obsolete,' because to get those new customers in, presumably you have to give them something fresh. This may go under the attractive name of keeping art vital and open to new talents, but to me it smacks of the usual notions that apply in retailing everywhere, which is that you have to keep renewing the product, declaring obsolescence." Heading in that direction, Susan often found herself growing "very cranky," and then inevitably taking on detractors of the canon, asking, "What's wrong with maintain-ing the canon? . . . Isn't there a difference between works of art and other products?" And the result? "[T]hey look at me pity-ingly as if I simply don't understand that yes, everything must be renewed, that nothing is exempt." Susan certainly under-stood, but remained, as she said, "radically unconvinced," believing "that what is on view here is an ideology that wraps a fundamentally commercial, economistic approach around the museum." For good reason, perhaps? Maybe, Susan would concede, while still wary of "the high-minded vocabulary" shrewdly deployed to conceal the fact that the so-called "appetites of the public" too often drive the major decisions that are made in the domain of arts and letters.

The charges leveled at Sontag and Steiner had often to do with their tone, erudition, and panache, which they did nothing to conceal, and even with what Joseph Epstein, editor of the *American Scholar,* called their "unremitting highbrowism."[22] George seemed to take inordinate pleasure in arguing that our faculties of responsiveness and understanding have "atrophied," that there are orders of difficulty in truly reading a demanding poem or novel, to which many of us are no longer equal. Once, at a 1992 New York State Summer Writers Institute craft discussion with students, I quoted a passage from George's essay "Text and Context" from 1975, and Susan agreed at once that many teachers and students went astray because they couldn't read very well. If this was true, Steiner wrote, then "we shall have to train them, explicitly, laboriously, in a setting inevitably besieged. . . . We shall have to become at once exceedingly modest and exceedingly arrogant in our *profession,* in the syllabus of our *calling.* . . . If we are serious about our business we shall have to teach *reading.* We shall have to teach it from the humblest level of rectitude, the parsing of a sentence, the grammatical diagnosis of a proposition, the scanning of a line of verse. . . . We will, simply, have to create universities or schools for reading."[23]

Sontag and Steiner were quintessentially *modern* intellectuals, jealous of their separateness and uniqueness, committed, like the modernist artists they admired, not to pandering to their audience but to challenging it. As cultural critic William Deresiewicz writes (in a 2021 *Salmagundi* interview), "the authentically modern self-defined itself against the group," whereas "the new self—the digital self—defines itself through affinity with the group. It is networked, not solitary; public, not inward. It wants to know who it's like, and who likes it."[24] In very different ways, Sontag and Steiner embodied a disciplined resistance to populist currents. Both were sometimes said to have been out of touch, though Susan had good reason to think the charge idiotic. It was obvious, even to George, that we now live in a culture dominated by the internet, where charges fly and land with a frequency previously unimaginable. Fortunately for them, neither paid much attention to a medium too often geared to the brief and the loud.

One of the first things I learned about George and Susan, once we became friends, was that they disliked and mistrusted one another, and marveled that I could find a way to be friends with a person as forbidding as each deemed the other to be. In fact, they saw one another only a few times, and then under my auspices, as I report in the course of this memoir. Those times produced a number of the most wrenching and hilarious moments of my life. But then almost everything about George and Susan was improbable. What the cultural critic Mark Greif wrote about Susan was largely applicable to George as well. "Susan," he wrote, "made you acknowledge that she was more intelligent than you." Likewise, George. "She then compelled you to admit that she felt more than you did." True, though perhaps not in the same degree for George. "She responded to art more vividly and completely. Not only her sense, but her sensibility, was grander." So, with George. Both were grand if by grand we mean that they didn't curry favor or make excuses for themselves or for anyone else. Grand, too, in their determination to "let you in on certain secrets: whom to read, how to gaze, what else there was to learn." Though both were very human, which is to say some of the time vulnerable and generous, neither inspired in me the slightest impulse to identify with them. They were too large, and the loathing they came to have for each other clearly had much to do with the sense that there was room on the current scene for only one such person.

My friendships with George Steiner and Susan Sontag were central to my life, and in part I've written this memoir to bear witness to their continuing importance as writers and thinkers. But I've wanted as well to make this a narrative rooted in a series of questions about friendship itself. In Joseph Joubert's *Notebooks* (1809), the French writer muses: "He must not only cultivate his friends, but cultivate his friendships within himself. They must be kept, cared for, watered."[25] That advice seems to me exactly right, and I can only hope that the record I've assembled here attests to that labor of cultivation and caring—and resistance.

Joubert also noted that "we always lose the friendship of those who lose our esteem." I'm not entirely sure how I won or kept the esteem of George and Susan. Affection, to be sure, even if in Susan's case it was decidedly unsteady. Esteem is harder to certify, the available tokens often unreliable; certainly my own esteem for George and Susan could never be doubted. Though I had reason to think about their flaws and frailties—I have much to say about them in this book—my admiration for what was best in them rarely faltered. Like them, I was always disposed to promote and celebrate my superiors, and in George and Susan I knew that I had found them.

ONE

---◆○▶---

The Fascination of What's Difficult: Susan Sontag

*"Sontag was accused of humorlessness, but in fact she was
guilty only of high-mindedness."*
JANET MALCOLM

*"[S]he manifested the older truth that all riveters of the mind-forged
manacles most fear . . . [that] one cannot
be just a little bit heretical."*
CHRISTOPHER HITCHENS

1 · SERIOUSLY UNCOOL?

THREE years after Susan Sontag died in December of 2004, Jenny Diski published in the *London Review of Books* an essay titled "Seriously Uncool." By that time Diski was not the only one who thought Sontag uncool, though I never entirely got over my sense of her as one of the coolest persons I'd ever met. I also never forgot that the word "cool" had a hundred different, often incompatible, meanings. When I wrote to Susan for the first time, in the spring of 1965, asking her to contribute an essay or review to a new magazine called *Salmagundi*, I thought her participation would confer on what we were doing a potent imprimatur—that she would ratify our ambition to be alert to the shock of the new. Though she would learn soon enough that I could never hope to be cool, she would forgive that deficit and embolden my thinking in a permanent and salutary way. If anyone had then said to me that Susan was "seriously uncool," I'd have replied at once that the word "uncool" could not possibly refer to someone so dazzling and volatile. She was, as Deborah Eisenberg wrote in the *New York Review of Books*, "at least twice as alive as most of us."[26] Sontag had a hunger to see and touch and taste even the most daunting and difficult things. She was equipped, moreover, not to be undone even by the most extravagant of sensations.

Though we had an occasional correspondence throughout the sixties, and I wrote my first essay about her ("On Susan Sontag and the New Sensibility") in 1966,[27] when I was twenty-four, we became friends only in 1974, when she agreed to sit for a public interview at Skidmore College. Even then I knew of others who believed she'd betrayed something they admired when she first burst upon the scene and became famous for her 1965 essay "Notes on 'Camp.'" By the mid-seventies friends of mine would speak of her as deadly serious and humorless, in spite of her gift for moving nimbly between high and low, mischievous and severe. But then I was never convinced that cool meant to others what it meant to me. Never convinced, for that matter, that the Susan Sontag I came to know could ever be "deadly." Words change, contexts change. Rick Moody said that the word cool went "from being meaningful to becoming hackneyed" in the course of the sixties, when "merchandisers and advertisers" got hold of it, and yet Susan remained, for some of us at least, as cool as she had ever been. Cool as in commanding, unapologetically opinionated, fabulously eloquent, irresistibly herself.

In "Against Cool," Moody observes that "if you have to talk about cool, you are not it,"[28] and that is one good reason why I never heard Susan use the word. She understood that as she became fashionable as an exemplar she might well cease to be cool. The danger of commodification was real, and I felt it for the first time when at a store across from the Pompidou Museum in Paris I bought several postcards bearing iconic photographs of Susan, ravishingly beautiful and serenely accessible. Were these images cool? Surely they would be regarded as such by the customers who purchased them and took the postcards home to pin up, or use as bookmarks, or mail to friends back in the states.

Still, it ought to have been obvious that what made Susan authentically cool was not principally her image or her beauty but her demeanor, the almost impossibly rigorous self-possession stamped on everything she wrote and in her every utterance. She was, after all, rigorous even about pleasure. She had little or no patience with those who wanted to relax. She wanted her pleasures rare and immoderate. In her presence, I felt my own impulses quicken. I felt smarter, more alert, poised to be contradicted, even undermined. I never doubted the force and ferocity of her will, never minded that to be in her company was to revolve around her. She was cool because she knew how to make conversation dangerous. There was no inclination in Susan towards the obvious or self-evident. Though she could be down to earth, even somewhat vulnerable, with those who were permitted to come close, she rarely let down her determination to be demanding. Cool was in her a perfect, unstudied resistance to banality and incoherence. Responsive to enigma and sublimity, she had no feeling for child's play or frivolity. She had her chosen masters but was always also masterful in the exercise of her own seductive powers.

In our thirty years of friendship Susan and I never used the word "cool" in conversation. No doubt she would have regarded it, as applied to her, as an unforgivable trivialization of everything she aspired to. If others continued to think of her as the embodiment of something merely smart and fashionable—surely she knew they did—well and good, so long as they didn't have the effrontery to suggest her importance had anything to do with that. To be cool, as both of us surely knew, was not always a welcome fate. It entailed, after all, a willing reduction to a posture, a refusal ever to acknowledge one's subordination to anything so ordinary as simple confusion, misgiving, or internal division. Or worse, to sentimentality or frailty.

Susan's early books, and even her later essays and speeches, have a disciplined resistance to misgiving. She spoke as one who had arrived at her judgments and conclusions with enviable certitude and more than ample exertion. Those who were not duly impressed disparaged the posture that prevented her from entertaining the doubts to which ordinary mortals might succumb.

The factors that made Sontag seem cool to her admirers are evident in her first book of essays, *Against Interpretation*. The combative title announced her opposition to the very thing most comfortable and familiar to literary academics. Interpretation was the meat and potatoes of the rank and file academic, who—like me—taught students to read literature in classrooms and usually grounded their own books in close readings of texts, canonical or otherwise. To thumb a nose at the earnest work of these practitioners was to open a way to an unfamiliar conception of the literary intellectual, who was now enjoined to become acutely responsive to an "erotics of art" and to artworks not only "advanced" but often perverse and destabilizing. Laugh all you want at persons who take themselves to be cool, but an earnest guy like me was no less susceptible to the allure of Susan's essays, and the glamor of their maker, than the multitudes of others who hoped she might teach them to be less conventional, cautious, and respectable than they were. Consider the following:

FROM *Against Interpretation*:

Jerking off the universe is perhaps what all philosophy, all abstract thought is about: an intense, and not very sociable pleasure, which has to be repeated again and again.

[T]he history of Camp taste is part of the history of snob taste. But since no authentic aristocrats in the old sense exist today to sponsor special tastes, who is the bearer of this taste? Answer: an improvised self-elected class, mainly homosexuals, who constitute themselves as aristocrats of taste.

FROM *Styles of Radical Will* (1968):

The art of our time is noisy with appeals for silence. A coquettish, even cheerful nihilism. One recognizes the imperative of silence, but goes on speaking any- way. Discovering that one has nothing to say, one seeks a way to say that.

One could plausibly argue that it is for quite sound reasons that the whole capacity for sexual ecstasy is inac- cessible to most people—given that sexuality is some- thing, like nuclear energy, which may prove amenable to domestication through scruple, but then again may not.

As Nietzsche wanted to will his moral solitude, Cio- ran wants to will the difficult. Not that the essays are hard to read, but their moral point, so to speak, is the unending disclosure of difficulty.[29]

What felt striking about such writing was its severity and freshness, its aura of indisputability and omniscience, its hau- teur and brio. Here were sentences written by someone who was—by nature it seemed—perfectly assertive. She moved for- ward with the almost frightening self-confidence of a writer who had considered everything and was unafraid of contradiction—if only because contradiction seemed to her petty and obtuse. Though she could be stung by the criticism of reviewers who ridiculed her ambition to be an avant-garde novelist or filmmaker, she rarely spoke of her vulnerability to attack, and once or twice, when she was moved to answer a critic, she could be scornful and withering—as in her memorable 1975 exchange in the *New York Review of Books* with Adrienne Rich, who had criticized Susan's "Fascinating Fascism." There Susan resorted to terms like "anti-intellectualism" and "infantile leftism" to characterize Rich's demand for a party-line adherence to so-called feminist solidarity. Why, Rich had asked, would a feminist writer like Susan undermine the claims to canonical status of a great woman artist like Leni Riefenstahl? Demands for solidarity, Sontag argued, read like a "kind of banal disparagement of the normative virtues of the intellect." What Rich promoted was a "rancid and dangerous antithesis between mind . . . and emotion." If Susan was shaken by the attack leveled by Rich, a writer she admired, she fired back with singular ferocity: "Party lines make for intellectual monotony and bad prose" and result in "demands for intellectual simplicity."[30]

The sometimes bruising declarativeness of Susan's sentences never came across as dull or earnest. Often the sentences were intended not so much to issue a verdict as to interrogate ideas—sometimes highly sophisticated ideas—that obstructed the painful truths she sought to uncover. When she began a sentence with "One could plausibly argue," you felt she wanted nothing less than that you change the way you thought. When she wrote in "The Third World of Women"—not reprinted in her early volumes—that "the modern 'nuclear' family is a psychological and moral disaster," "a prison of sexual repression . . . a museum of possessiveness, a guilt-producing factory, and a school of selfishness," she was not earnestly contending for plausibility and reasonableness but giving herself permission to be excessive, brash, peremptory.[31] No trace of the caution that figures so prominently in the writing of critics looking to win a consensus.

My own inveterate earnestness—so I always told myself—did not prevent me from doing what was necessary, earning my way onto enemies lists, going against the grain of standard academic practice, and taking on intellectual opponents more established than I could ever be. In truth, Susan didn't often do anything to dislodge that impression. Though she did often complain that I was "too nice," and wished I could "get over that," we remained friends, in part because she thought me combative enough, and liked my appetite for controversy.

What always struck and amused her was how fabulously uncool I was. No doubt this had something to do with my marriage, with the fact that whenever we arranged to be together our "together" would mean "the Boyers," Peg and Robert. Only two or three times in thirty years did we see one another one on one, and when we'd talk about marriage she would invariably come out with something like "Of course I'm not speaking about the two of you" or "That's not a model of marriage for anyone else" or "Really you don't get bored spending all that time together?" She never let on that she craved anything remotely like the uncool relationship Peg and I had, though I learned from accounts of her early marriage to Philip Rieff that there was a closeness between them and an intimacy in working together that she missed when it was gone.

Susan was, for all the aura of unanswerable mastery she conveyed, completely unpredictable. Her intensity had nothing in common with the IT conveyed by the Beat writers, their ambition to be, as Kerouac wrote, "cruising in the neon glories of the new American night."[32] Susan's adrenaline flow was surely a match for theirs, but there was rarely anything idle in her outlook. When we went with five or six writers to the old Adelphi Hotel in Saratoga Springs late on a Summer Writers' Institute night, after a reading or panel discussion, and laughed, and reminisced just a little, there was always the prospect that Susan would turn on a remark one of us had made, remind us that even on such a night, in such a setting, she might pounce and correct and challenge. Her capacity for spontaneity made us all alert to the prospect that she might suddenly erupt in a way that could seem exhilarating or frightening.

On a mild July night in 1995 Susan suddenly recalled that months earlier, after an event at the 92nd Street Y in Manhattan, Peg and I had "inexplicably" rushed off to catch a late-night train, thus leaving her to dine alone with our mutual friend Nadine Gordimer.

"But Susan," Peg said, "Nadine knew we came down that afternoon so Robert could introduce her at her reading, and we agreed that we would spend two quiet hours together in the Green Room of the Y beforehand. There was no surprise, no sudden departure. Nadine felt bad only that we'd have the four hours of late-night travel so that Robert could teach an early-morning class at Skidmore the next day."

"But that's just it," Susan went on, looking now for support from Bharati Mukherjee and one or two other friends, all seated somewhat bewildered at the Adelphi Hotel table. "You didn't care, apparently, that Nadine had traveled not from upstate New York but from Johannesburg, and couldn't possibly have expected you would rush off that way."

"I'm sure Nadine loved having you all to herself at dinner," I replied, "and the letter she sent me a week later from Johannesburg emphasized how perfectly our plan worked."

"Well," said Susan, with an aggrieved finality I'd heard often enough before, "you always tell yourself what you want to believe."

Nothing "cool" in that sort of eruption, Susan's composure unstable. On another evening, when Susan and I were talking about the susceptibility of women to being silenced, or just mildly going along with their men, I mentioned several classic Hollywood movies, suggesting that they contradicted ideas about conventional images of women and the way those ideas had been sold in the popular culture.

"Oh, I'm not talking about those kinds of movies," Susan said. "And besides, I don't think I've seen most of them, and wouldn't want to."

"Oh, come on," I countered. "I bet you'd laugh your head off if we watched some of them together. And you'd be stunned at the kinds of things the women in those films get to say. The put-downs directed at the sometimes-hapless men, the fact that in the best of the movies, those starring Katherine Hepburn and Bette Davis, for example, the women are usually smarter and quicker than the men."

"And so, you're saying," Susan replied, "that we've got it all wrong, and that all we have to do is watch the movies that millions were watching in the thirties and forties to have a proper view of gender relations?"

"I'm only saying," I added, "that the attitudes we think derive from mass culture actually derive, maybe to a much greater degree, from other sources."

On that occasion Susan backed away, just a bit, from what might have become a real argument, largely, I assumed, because she was indifferent to the kinds of movies I was citing. In principle, indifferent. Her sense of herself, and of what mattered and deserved to matter, required that she not further engage with those movies. Not venture in the direction of things apt to be unworthy.

Often Susan could not help herself, erupting when she might have wished to remain aloof. Lost her cool not by seeming less authoritative, less peremptory, but by allowing herself to seem discomfited, even undone. One of the more bizarre episodes in our long relationship occurred in July 1999, when I introduced her to an audience at the New York State Summer Writers Institute, as I had done on July evenings for over a decade. As always, I referred to her in my introduction as "Susan." And as expected she gave a reading from her new novel, *In America*, and fielded audience questions before heading to a reception across campus. All sane and predictable throughout the subsequent book signing and casual socializing with the Institute faculty, standing around and kibitzing. Though the fee was less than paltry, Susan never refused my annual invitation to speak at the summer institute, where she drew a large crowd and clearly enjoyed participating in a program where her son, David Rieff, and old friends like Richard Howard were faculty members. Usually she stayed on for a few days before heading back to Manhattan, and though she never drew close to other faculty like Marilynne Robinson, Robert Pinsky, or Frank Bidart, she liked trying out new work and conversing with the writers assembled at the Boyers dining table each weeknight, a little incredulous at my helping a student assistant clear the table and hand around dessert before we all departed for the 8 p.m. public event on the Skidmore College campus. Most often her mood was lighthearted on those summer evenings, and in 1999 she was clearly excited and encouraged by the first reviews of *In America*.

But one night, after a public reading, when we got into our car with Susan, her Italian translator Paolo Di Leonardo, and two other writers, Susan at once opened up on me, and continued relentlessly through two hours in the garden at the rear of the Adelphi Hotel. The charge? That I had consistently referred to her as "Susan" in my introduction that night. Did I not hear how wrong that was, to belittle her "in front of an audience of strangers"? Did I not hear how "disrespectful" that had to sound to people who didn't know either of us and had no idea we were friends? She was sure I would never have referred to Seamus Heaney or other poets I admired by their first names. Had I been asked to introduce Yehudi Menuhin before a concert I'd not have referred to him as "Yehudi." I'd surely have used "Maestro" or some other honorific. She too had a right to expect that I would know better than to introduce her to an audience by her first name.

"Why," she asked, "do you sit there looking so astonished? Have I said anything astonishing?"

"I'm astonished," I said, "for one thing, because I've always introduced you as Susan and you've never complained before."

"I'm sure that isn't true," she said.

"But it is," I replied, "and tomorrow morning I'll be happy to play a tape of your evening at the institute from last year, and the year before."

"I know you're wrong about that," Susan persisted. "But even if it was so, what would that prove? The point is that tonight you couldn't hear how wrong it was to call me 'Susan.'"

"And you, dear Susan," Peg Boyers then quietly added, "can't hear how unpleasant it is to hear you carrying on about this, when it's so . . . so small and unnecessary."

"It may be unnecessary," Susan said, "but it isn't small, is it? Do you think it's small?" she asked our friend Bharati Mukherjee.

"I think everyone in that auditorium understood that the

two of you have been friends for a long time," Bharati answered, "and that it's natural for Bob to call you Susan. That it would have felt wrong for him to call you something else. Definitely not 'Maestro.'"

We got over this altercation after a half hour or so of pointless and petty wrangling, and by the next morning, when we arrived to take Susan and the others to breakfast, she declared that I must never, ever call her anything but Susan, no matter the company, no matter the setting. The following day she phoned from Manhattan and apologized again, and a month later she and Peg exchanged letters.

"You were so sweet to worry about having given Robert a hard time," Peg wrote in a September letter. But it was hard not to think, then and later, as at numbers of earlier times, that Susan had been anything but cool. For all of her conviction of always being in the right, she could sometimes be bullying and speak with a surprising and disappointing lack of self-awareness. Though I forgave her, I wondered at the display of harshness and entitlement coming from a person who could be generous and anything but petty.

I never ceased to think of cool as potentially a virtue, though I know that cool people often want too much to be noticed for their difference. Susan didn't have to try to open herself to what others disdained. Her catholicity of taste was genuine. She had an appetite for rock music and for Tchaikovsky, for opera and a shoe museum. She did also take pleasure in reminding us that she was really very different. That she didn't own a television set. Wouldn't. That she occasionally hung out with people most of her friends would not want to have anything to do with. That she traveled to dangerous places, including war-torn Sarajevo in the nineties, while all around weapons were being fired and bombs were exploding. However much Susan had to be aware of the image she projected, she was so thoroughly invested in her appetites and projects that I never doubted she was one of the coolest persons I had ever known. That was one reason I was so disappointed on those occasions when she exhibited a side of herself that was decidedly unappealing.

2 · IS THIS RUDE?

HANGING on the wall of a brownstone in the Bedford Stuyvesant district of Brooklyn is a framed 2001 photograph of Susan with her arm thrown about the shoulder of our youngest son, Gabe. He and his husband, Drew, have had that photo on their wall for at least a dozen years. In some ways, it seems to us among the best of the photos assembled there, though it is a snapshot, taken with an ordinary camera by Peg at a quiet, intimate breakfast, the morning after a public reading attended by several hundred people. What stands out is Susan's expression of sheer, uncomplicated pleasure in the company of a young man she had known as a boy, who had suddenly become interesting in a new and unexpected way. The two fond companions look straight ahead, no trace of unease or reluctance inscribed on their faces, no thought just then of the dozens of people lining up nearby to have "Ms. Sontag" autograph their books. Gabe was twenty, Susan just past seventy.

Susan had a surprising capacity for affection—"surprising" because she could be, much of the time, abrasive and condescending. When we showed her the photograph at her apartment a month or two after it was taken, she was giddy, almost girlish in her enthusiasm. I didn't think I could look that good any more, she said. A tribute to the photographer. And Gabe, she went on, he looks even younger than he seems when you meet him, though once he opens up his mouth you feel that he's formidable. It's something, isn't it, she said, her eyes fixed on the photograph, to have sons like your Gabe and my David. Friends. People you can talk to, who don't make you feel you want to flee and find someone else. But then you know, don't you, that you've made him, that it didn't just happen. That's what I sometimes think about when I'm standing next to David and I hear those sentences of his roll out.

We never learned whether Susan kept or hung the photograph we delivered to her that day, though she referred to it on several occasions when she asked us about Gabe: Might she see those poems he had written? Would he perhaps be playing his violin at a concert venue in Manhattan so we could go together to watch him play? Did we regard him increasingly as a friend? A best friend?

We were not alone among Susan's friends in feeling that she was more than curious about our family members. When we were together, six or seven times over the course of each year, she had all sorts of intimate questions, and about Gabe especially she grew more and more inquisitive once he'd come out and spoken with her about it. Destined for a career as a musician and a rare book and art dealer, Gabe was almost a match for her in his hunger for art and ideas, and she thought him interesting in ways that differentiated him from his parents.

Susan's correspondence with Peg was very occasional, and never included the kinds of conflict and tension that sometimes marked my own relations with Susan. A mutual friend said it was clear she just liked Peg better, and finished with "Who wouldn't?" In the summer of 1990, when Susan's son, David Rieff, was teaching nonfiction at our July Summer Writers Institute, and Susan had just left us after a two-day visit, Peg wrote to say how much she missed her. But she wanted also to say that her seventy-year-old Cuban mother was enrolled in David's class, learning how to shape the memoir-cookbook that eventually appeared as *A Taste of Old Cuba*. "Don't worry about David," Peg wrote. "He's a hit with his students, as far as I can tell. My mother's in love. That's certain. And he's writing away—fiendishly typing and faxing. . . . It's not easy to know exactly what's going on with David. . . . He is very special and one wants always to be worthy somehow."

That remained a foundation for Peg and Susan: their feeling for one another's sons and for their mutuality as anxious mothers. But then they had other concerns as well. In 1986, when Susan's great story, "The Way We Live Now," appeared in the *New Yorker*, she sent Peg an advance copy. Peg wrote her at once: "I know the story must have come from somewhere very deep; it feels so true. Only someone who's had cancer, who's been there, could have written such a story." Of course, she went on, "the atmosphere of panic" in the story called most obviously to mind what was then unfolding in the lives of AIDS victims and their friends. But the important thing was to say thank you for writing this, and "brava di nuovo."

While "The Way We Live Now" brought Susan mail from all over the world, she wrote to Peg, "I'm elated by your words. Your praise means a great deal to me. When you say that you know the story must have come from somewhere very deep, that only someone who had cancer, who's been there could have written this story—you're right. I treasure your making that comment, which is one that only one other person has said to me—Nadine Gordimer. Most people think it's a story about AIDS. Of course, AIDS is what the unnamed patient at the center of the story has. But, as you and Nadine saw, it's not a story about AIDS."

Peg enormously valued such exchanges with Susan, and there was never a time when she didn't feel close and concerned about her.

Susan's attention, even to close friends and their families, could be unstable and unreliable. Often, when we were speaking with others who knew Susan, we would laugh and say that with her it was clearly "out of sight, out of mind." No doubt she had stronger attachments to a handful of selected others, and none of us ever blamed her for inconstancy. When we phoned, and made an appointment, she was always ready to see us, and once we got together she made us feel that no one could ever have been more important to her. She did occasionally go out of her way to assure us that her friends included especially important people: A-list celebrities, performers, musicians, actors, and Nobel prize winners. Even early in our friendship, it seemed to me that I was deemed worthy in part because I too had friendships with "important" writers and thinkers, some of whom she gained access to through conferences and symposia I sponsored at Skidmore College.

Like most intellectuals of my acquaintance, Susan loved gossip, and she clearly got off on the gossip we could provide about people she thought a good deal more interesting than Peg or me. "About your April shindig," she wrote Peg in March 1987, "I'm keen to come and watch the glamorous people babble." The shindig was a three-day conference on "Race, Religion and Nationalism," and the babblers included George Steiner, Conor Cruise O'Brien, Kwame Anthony Appiah, and a dozen other intellectuals. All of them thought Susan herself the most "glamorous" of those we assembled, though the atmosphere of that three days was colored somewhat by threats emanating from the Irish Republican Army, phoned in to the office of Skidmore College President David Porter, who was warned to see to it that the "enemy of the Irish people," my former teacher Conor Cruise O'Brien, not be kept on our program as keynote speaker and participant. Though nothing came of the repeated IRA threats, four armed policeman stood guard at the rear of the college auditorium throughout the three days of the meeting, O'Brien himself long accustomed to such threats.

It was never easy to know when Susan would find someone boring. Though she enjoyed attention, including the sustained attention of an audience inclined to drink in every syllable she uttered, she also dreaded the aftermath of public events, when she'd be required to pretend she wanted to hear what an audience member or autograph seeker had to say. On a July evening, as we strolled to a reception across campus from a large Skidmore College facility where she'd been feted on many previous July evenings at the Summer Writers Institute, she said, "Please don't let all those people have at me, and please just have Gabe sit next to me and talk my ear off so that I won't have to look up and let those other people spoil my evening." Soon she drew Gabe to her in the cozy booth she'd selected and refused to acknowledge any of the many students enrolled in the program who had lined up for a moment of her attention. "Is this rude," she asked me, "to just ignore them as if they weren't there?"

"Sure, it's rude," I assured her, "but you can make them wait for a while if you want to have your time with Gabe before acknowledging them."

Susan was often rude and could be breathtakingly nasty, even to people close to her. To me, certainly, and even to older friends like Richard Howard. We all tolerated this behavior simply because we knew her to be a person of moods and seizures. Strange to think of her as out of control or helpless to do anything about what came over her, but there it was. Often Peg would say that Susan was off her meds or in need of a new prescription.

Few people were prepared to tell Susan to fuck off when she was behaving badly. Rarely did she pay a price for her more intemperate outbursts. There was so much about her to like and admire that her friends didn't want to do anything that might end the friendship. Who would be willing to renounce any further hours with one of the most compelling persons you'd ever met? Who would not be willing to absorb some punishment, even humiliation, if the alternative was to lose her completely?

Of course, not everyone Susan met knew who she was or what she had to offer. In truth, she was an equal opportunity ball buster. Her rudeness was not solely reserved for people equipped to forgive her or to tolerate her on behalf of her indisputable virtues of heart and intellect. Customarily courteous to waiters and waitresses, she could turn savagely on a serving person who had brought her an undercooked meal or neglected to put out the condiments she had requested. Was that too harsh, she might ask us, to which we would say, Probably, but not a big deal.

One of the most explosive encounters triggered by Susan's imperiousness occurred on an evening in Manhattan when we were to pick her up at her Chelsea apartment and take her to dinner at a downtown Indian restaurant. It was a foul April night, marked by a drenching rain.

"You should have a raincoat," I told her as we were about to leave the apartment.

"I won't need one," Susan said. "We'll grab a taxi as soon as we step out onto Twenty-Third Street."

But in fact, we didn't manage at once to get a cab, and I got thoroughly wet, hopelessly waving my arm at the "occupied" missiles of taxis cruising past me while Susan and Peg sheltered at the front door of Susan's building.

Grateful at last to be settled into a cab after perhaps ten minutes out in the driving rain, I called out the address of the restaurant, and the driver said, Fine. I know where it is, right off Seventh Avenue, at which Susan said, "Let me handle this, Robert," and proceeded, from her seat next to our driver, to assure him that she'd been to this address many times and would direct him exactly.

"Not a problem," said the driver. "I'll just turn here onto Ninth Avenue."

"No, you won't do that," said Susan. "You see, right away I can tell you have no idea what you're doing or where you're going."

"Well then," said the driver, "why don't you tell me what you have in mind?"

"What I have in mind," she repeated, her voice suddenly quivering with exasperation. "It's not what I have in mind. It's simply the route we need to take. And if you don't keep talking back to me, we can get somewhere. And so, don't turn onto Ninth but drive east and go downtown on Seventh."

"I can do that," said the driver, "but you know this is rush hour, and Seventh is impossible downtown at this time, not to mention the construction that blocks the avenue after Eighteenth Street."

"Can you believe this?" Susan asked us. "Who does this man think he is? Here," she said, turning back to the driver seated next to her, "I'm giving you instructions and you are challenging me as if I had to get your permission. Can't you hear that I'm ordering you to go the way I'm telling you to go? Do you understand the word 'ordering'? Have you ever been given an order and just followed it? Or are you incapable of keeping your mouth shut and just doing what you're told?"

A moment later the three of us were out on the sidewalk, trucks concussing the air, the rain heavy, our one mid-size umbrella woefully inadequate, the wind threatening to turn the thing inside out. Our taxi driver had done what seemed to me the right thing by stopping the moment Susan uttered the words "keeping your mouth shut," and then reaching across Susan to open her door. "Out," he said, first quietly, and then, when Susan said, "You can't be serious," with much greater menace, "Out of my taxi this second, all of you."

In my decades of friendship with Susan, I witnessed many an altercation prompted by her abrasive temper, though I never saw anyone else handle the situation with the impressive and decisive aplomb of our taxi driver. No doubt others came close to telling her off, or worse, but resisted the temptation for reasons that must have seemed compelling.

Shortly after the publication of her novel *The Volcano Lover* in July 1992, she agreed to be interviewed by a journalist from the *Albany Times Union* in the editorial offices of *Salmagundi*. Though a day earlier I'd told Susan she could change her mind, she decided to go forward with the interview, "as long as you sit right outside the door and save me when you think I've had enough." The journalist was a young woman, perhaps thirty, in a business suit and tie, clearly thrilled with her assignment and eager to please, though from the first minute of their encounter I knew things would not go well.

"Were you surprised by *Volcano*?" Susan asked as the young woman took her seat across the desk.

"You mean the novel *The Volcano Lover*," said the woman, "which I intend to read but can't say that I have."

"Robert," Susan at once called to me, so that I came in and found Susan already standing behind my desk, glaring at the reporter. "This person asked to interview me and hasn't read *Volcano*, so that I can't imagine what she hopes to accomplish here. Perhaps, with you present, she can tell me what she knows and doesn't know. So tell me—you're a reporter, right?—which of my books have you read?"

"I read 'Notes on "Camp"' for a class of mine a few years ago," the young woman said, "and just the other day I bought a copy of *On Photography*, though I haven't had a chance to open it. But I did have some general questions to ask you."

"General questions," Susan intoned. "What are general questions? Do you know what general questions are, Robert? It sounds to me like the questions you resort to when you are totally ignorant and totally unprepared for the assignment. Would you agree," she went on, standing and glaring still at the young woman, whose eyes had fallen and who seemed to be gripping the book bag she had brought with her and placed on the desk, "would you agree that you are in fact completely unprepared to do an interview with me? Do you have any idea who I am? Do you know anything about my work, that I've been at it for thirty years and that some people think it worth reading?"

"Yes, I suppose I am unprepared," said the journalist. "And I hate to upset you. I didn't think I would upset you."

"No, no, you didn't upset me," said Susan. "Don't believe for a minute that you could upset me. But do me the favor at least of asking me a general question so I know what you thought you'd do for an hour this morning."

"I was going to ask you about your background."

"My background where?"

"Well, I don't know where you grew up, and that was why I thought it would be a good question."

"And what else by way of a general question?"

"Well, I thought I'd ask you if you've changed your view of anything in the years since you wrote 'Notes on "Camp."'"

"Which views would you think I might have changed," Susan replied, seated now and darting bemused glances in my direction as I stood transfixed at the open office door, taking it all in.

"Well, I don't know which views, but I thought they might have changed, and if they did, I thought you would be willing to tell me."

"Actually, I'm not willing to tell you anything, and I'm appalled that a reputable newspaper would send someone so totally ignorant to waste my time. So why don't you gather up your briefcase, or whatever it is, and drive back to wherever you came from, and try to remember, for the rest of your life, what a real journalist needs to do. Can you do that?"

"I think I can. And I do understand," the journalist said, as she timidly shook my hand and disappeared. Susan shot me the knowing, superior smirk of an accomplice who, with me as a silent presiding presence, had managed somehow to do who knows what: To uphold a standard? Get the day off on a properly harsh and didactic note? Hard to say. Nothing to complain about, I felt, in Susan's unkind behavior. Her haughty interrogation of the witless reporter was, under the circumstances, a characteristic performance. The reporter had seen Susan as she often was, a gift she might treasure, or quickly teach herself to forget. Of course, I could not have summoned the will to obliterate such a person; I lacked the righteous anger required to humiliate someone who clearly deserved to be called out and sent packing. In retrospect, I thought Susan's controlled fury at once impressive and scary. The sort of thing you did, and did again, only if you were not much inclined ever to think about what the drive home might have been like for the person you had humiliated.

3 · DISAPPOINTMENTS AND DISMISSALS

Now and then we talked about what was and wasn't infuriating, or boring. "No," she said once, "whatever you may think, I've never found you boring. At least never boring so that I want to scream."

"You remember," I said, "that once you told me my remarks to an audience member were too polite. Anemic. You said you don't like anemic."

"It's not always a matter of liking or not liking," she said. "Much of the time it's just what I can stand to be put through. I know, because I've seen you under fire," she said, "that you don't mind being argued with. Boring and anemic people can't stand to be argued with. Of course, you don't most of the time want to argue with me."

"Well," I said, "I do contradict you now and then."

"Very rarely," Susan said.

In 1996 Susan was invited to deliver a lecture at Rensselaer Polytechnic Institute (RPI) in Troy, New York, forty-five minutes or so from Saratoga Springs, and phoned to ask if Peg and I might fetch her after the lecture and bring her to our home for a couple of days. Her hosts had set up a dinner after the lecture, but already she had told them that she would skip the dinner and attend the reception only for fifteen minutes or so. She was delighted with herself for having made this arrangement clear to her hosts, and she knew that either Peg or I would be willing to "save" her, as we had done on other occasions.

By the time we got Susan into the car that night in Troy it was almost ten o'clock, and she was ravenous. With few night-time options in our upstate area, we ended up in an all-night diner. Though Susan was often very particular about the restaurants she selected, she was oddly delighted with this place, ordered a burger and fries, and soon went on about how comfortable the seating was, and how terrific it was that such places continued to stay open all night. After about an hour, Peg mentioned that she must be "exhausted" after traveling earlier in the day from Manhattan, but Susan insisted that, as far as she was concerned, this would be an ideal place to just hang out and talk, no one else around to overhear us. "Maybe you're too tired," she said to Peg. But no, Peg assured her, we were perfectly willing to stay on for a while and order another dessert.

At first the conversation focused on Susan's hosts at RPI.

"Nice people," she said, "though the student questions after the lecture were disappointing, and you could tell they weren't well prepared. Hadn't been assigned anything. Just told to show up, no sense that this was disrespectful. Didn't you think so?"

"I don't know," I said. "Sometimes you think that just getting them to come out for an event is accomplishment enough, and you tell yourself they'll get something from the lecture, and from the give and take afterwards, even if they come in knowing very little about what to expect."

"That's what comes from long years of teaching undergraduates," Susan said. "Your own expectations are lowered, and soon you can't imagine anything better than a mildly respectful audience absorbing a small fraction of what's offered."

"You sound a bit like the George Steiner you always complain about," I suddenly said. "The Steiner who says that American undergraduate education is organized amnesia, to which I've heard you say that as usual he exaggerates and makes sweeping generalizations. And yet your own view isn't different at all, is it? You resent as much as he does that students don't read anything, and aren't made to feel their inadequacy. One reason why you don't care to teach, and certainly not undergraduates."

Susan hated to be compared to Steiner, though now and then she conceded that in several respects they were both exemplars of something rare in American intellectual life. At a 1979 *Salmagundi* conference on "Art and Intellect in America," Susan had declared, when Steiner was under attack from several prominent writers, that Steiner thinks "there are great works of art, which are clearly superior to anything else in their various forms, that there is such a thing as profound seriousness. And works created out of profound seriousness have in his view a claim on our attention and loyalty that surpasses qualitatively and quantitatively any claim made by any other form of art or entertainment." Were there many American literary people who would sign on to such a view? She didn't think so. In fact, she said that there were those, especially in the American academy, who were all too ready to reach for "the dismissive adjective 'elitist'" to describe such a stance, whereas Susan herself was more than willing to associate herself with Steiner's commitment to "seriousness." That was the virtue she admired more than any other, and rarely found.

The 1996 late-night exchange in the diner about the lines of affinity between Steiner and Susan was a laughing matter. For a while at least. When reminded of her own ambivalences and shifts in perspective, Susan could be generous and even amused. But then she felt compelled to turn the tables and ask how someone (me) who professed to care about her and Steiner could also be welcoming to writers who were anything but serious. Did she not see, in an advertisement we'd run in the *New York Review of Books* only a week or so earlier, that the participants in the New York State Summer Writers Institute included not only her and several other major writers but frauds like "the unspeakable Jay McInerney"? Was I not embarrassed to place such a person on the list of faculty slated to teach in my program? Surely I didn't believe that McInerney had anything remotely to do with the profound seriousness she had always thought I was committed to?

By no means a ridiculous question and one I'd heard before from Susan, even though she had made a name for herself by proposing that intellectuals learn to lighten up and have fun. She wanted to be more open and generous than she was. She had an appetite for the new mainly when the new was hard to swallow, and she was invariably disdainful about anything that looked like merely competent journeyman work. McInerney was a successful and popular writer and, therefore, suspect. Undergrads who had no appetite for serious reading, she believed, were fans of *Bright Lights, Big City* and wanted to write like the guy who had it in him to turn out such a book. Worse, McInerney was a writer who made it into gossip columns and hung out with beautiful people who would never have read a book by the writers Susan revered—by W. G. Sebald or Roland Barthes or Danilo Kis. To have placed his name on a roster that included authors like Marilynne Robinson and Louise Glück was a form of disrespect to the real writers on the list, and no doubt McInerney himself knew he was lucky to be placed in that company.

"What have you read by McInerney?" I asked Susan. "I mean, have you read anything by him, or do you know him by reputation only?"

"Some writers you don't have to read to know what they're about," Susan quipped, and laughed, partly at herself and her breezy way of trying to deflect the direct question. "It's not as if there isn't plenty of information about him out there," she went on. "You sound as if I have only to read him to change my mind completely. Is that it? Well I did read *Bright Lights*, and alright, it was a promising young man's book. Did you think it was better than that?"

"It was," I said, "much better than that. The sentences are terrific."

"You wouldn't want to write such a book," Susan quipped.

"Well, for starters, I couldn't. Don't have those sentences in me to write. And I would never have wanted the experience of New York City fast-lane life that drives such a book. As you know, I don't do drugs and I don't care to hang out with people who are perpetually high or wanting to be. No one would ever mistake me for one of the beautiful people."

"There's no interior life in McInerney's characters," Susan jabbed. "I can't see why anyone would want to spend four or five hours in their company."

"I should probably be ashamed of myself to say it—to say it to you, at any rate—but I remember my hours in that company with pleasure. I even remember feeling a bit of envy. For the sheer vitality of the thing, even the wit, and for the window into a world I would prefer to know only as a reader."

"I bet you haven't read anything else by him."

"Not true, not true. After all, he comes to the institute each summer, draws lots of students who want to study with him, and on one night each summer I get to introduce him. So that I have to read his latest books when they come out."

"Don't tell me you'd write a glowing review of any one of them."

"But I would, I would. I'd have all sorts of praise for his novel *The Last of the Savages.*"

"And then why didn't you ask Leon Wieseltier to let you review it for the *New Republic?*"

"It occurred to me, but then Leon was sending me other kinds of books to review. Books that you would be more likely to approve of. Difficult books. Peter Handke. Norman Manea. László Krasznahorkai. European writers mainly."

"So you think I should read the *Savages* novel?"

"You won't like it. You're disposed not to. And you'll blame me if you waste your time on it."

We often had this kind of mild quarrel, and in some ways, it was the most appealing aspect of our long friendship. I was grateful that Susan allowed me to contradict her, but wondered why I should be so grateful. Probably because we enjoyed the fun of such repartee, though occasionally this banter could take a turn towards something harsher and deeper. More than once this turnabout occurred when our friend Leonard Michaels was around, as he was each summer when he taught at the Writers Institute. Lennie was one of the American writers I most admired, and I was thrilled when he agreed to teach for us each July over six years of the nineties. Susan had praised his stories from the time he published his second volume, *I Would Have Saved Them If I Could.* On the paperback edition were her words: "A dense, ribald, astringent outpouring of pure talent. . . . Leonard Michaels's new collection will break your heart and make you laugh." A perfect encomium. When I got to know Lennie, he seemed at once the guy who had written the very hot stories that, as another writer once said, didn't ever cool down.

When I told Susan one night at a Turkish restaurant on the West Side that Lennie had agreed again to teach for us in the summer program, she rolled her eyes, and hoped she wouldn't have to be there when he was in residence.

"Did you have a fight?" I asked.

"No," Susan replied, "it was much worse than that." She retained an old affection for Lennie, she assured me, but now felt depressed whenever she saw him, which wasn't often. After all, "he had been so promising, and now was clearly not," she said. "He was, who knew what to call it?" At any rate, he hadn't written anything first-rate in a while, and it was obvious that he had nothing left. His novel *The Men's Club* was proof positive that nothing important was to be expected from him. "And that's depressing, isn't it? A big talent like that gone to ruin."

None of what Susan said about Lennie seemed accurate. You had only to read one or two of his most recent stories to see that he was far from finished. Had she read them? It was obvious, Susan said, that there was a decline. That he was running on empty. "What about the journals he was publishing in *Salmagundi* and that were appearing in other magazines? There is nothing like them," I said.

"They're emotionally played out," Susan corrected. "The deadpan is formulaic."

"I don't know," I said. "It all feels strangely alive to me. Feral and sensual. Even the suicides and the rages. The fragmented record of a guy tallying up his losses, alert to the danger of expressing love. Maybe if I didn't know and admire the stories so much I wouldn't think as well of the diaries."

"Didn't someone compare the neurotic *shtick* in the diaries to the terminal self-absorption of the characters in *Seinfeld*?" Susan quipped.

"Completely off," I said." I mean, there's nothing remotely lacerating in *Seinfeld*. Though you've probably never seen *Seinfeld*."

"Look," Susan said, "there's your friend Lennie, and then there's Canetti."

"I love Canetti as much as you do," I replied.

"But those diaries, or journals, *The Torch in My Ear*, *The Tongue Set Free*," Susan countered, "there's nothing to compare with them. Every entry in Canetti feels like the fruit of a lifetime's reflection. Nothing fragmentary, nothing just caught on the wing. Lennie's quick and smart, and he goes very deep, but he's not a philosopher."

"I get it," I conceded. "Once you say Canetti, or Gide, well, what writers like that make of their obsessions is more than even I would claim for Lennie. The comparison with Canetti somehow seems to me wrong. Not unfair but somehow wrong. Their sensibilities are too different."

"But don't you find Lennie much of the time embarrassing? He's always attractive, always coming out with something that makes you want to listen, for just a second or two. Then you think there's not much there. That he's exhausted his material. There's something soft and familiar in what he does. As I say, embarrassing."

"But why embarrassing?" I pushed back. "Even if you don't think much of the work, I don't get what would seem embarrassing. Or soft. The journals are harrowing."

"He takes too much pleasure in parading his penchant for mischief. For dissatisfaction. There's too much of the can't get no satisfaction in the writing. Something desperate and, at the same time, a little pathetic. I always feel uncomfortable being around him when I think he's the man who wrote *The Men's Club*. I had such hopes for him. How about you, Peg? You don't find him a little pathetic?"

"I love being around him," Peg said. "I like the way he is

with his daughter, and the new work he's been reading to us each summer is, I don't know, electric."

"I think you like him," Susan said, "because he's always very courtly with beautiful women. Admit it, Peg. Don't you think he's always coming on to you, even with Robert right there next to you?"

"He doesn't need to come on to me," Peg said. "He has all those younger women in his class to throw themselves at him. And he and Robert have a very sweet relationship."

"You've trained yourself not to notice," Susan said. "You tell yourself that he's fatherly with his daughter and wouldn't think of doing anything to annoy Robert. But I've seen him with good looking women."

"Anyway," I said, "it isn't that sort of thing that makes you feel embarrassed to be in Lennie's company. And I'm sure there were times when you felt Lennie coming on to you."

"Maybe a long time ago," Susan said. "But not lately."

"And so why embarrassed?" I persisted.

"Maybe because I put my money on him. Because I let everyone know I thought he was the real thing, and he isn't."

"You're embarrassed because he let you down?" I asked. "Because you think he made you look bad?"

"Now you're saying it's all about my vanity," Susan said. "Don't look surprised. That's what you're saying."

"If the shoe fits," I replied. "I mean I'm just asking. And you know, it's more than embarrassment that you gave off when you were around Lennie last summer. I've seen that sort of thing with you before. Especially when you have David with you and you both look like you've decided to make Lennie or some other has-been feel irrelevant. Like he doesn't exist, not for either of you anyway."

"Don't tell me you think Lennie picks up any of that," Susan said.

"He picks up that you don't think of him the way you used to."

"I'm sure he never complained to you about that."

"He wouldn't complain," I said. "But he's capable of feeling lousy about it, and wondering what the hell it's all about."

"And what did you mean when you said that my bad behavior is most noticeable when my David is around? You never told me that before."

"It's nothing other people haven't noted," I said. "David can be pretty condescending on his own, and when he picks up on a certain tendency in you, to recoil from someone, he's all over it. The two of you together can give off a powerful blast of disdain. Others have felt it often enough. Not only Lennie."

Though Susan was poised now and then to show me the sort of disapproval she exhibited towards others, she clearly liked that I talked back to her when we were not on a public platform performing for others. She never quite acknowledged that her embarrassment about Lennie Michaels had much to do with her vanity, or her wish to be right about everything and to pronounce verdicts without being second-guessed. But we got through most of our intimate exchanges without acrimony.

One mutual friend Susan liked to talk about was Charles Newman. He founded the magazine *Tri-Quarterly* around the time I began *Salmagundi,* in the mid-1960s. He was a promising novelist with several nonfiction books to his credit, and though Susan never thought him more than promising, she found him enormously attractive, possibly the most beautiful man she'd ever met. She liked his manner, his wry disparagement of academics, and his taste in writers. He had put together special issues of his magazine on avant-garde writers like Borges and Nabokov, and he championed thinkers like E. M. Cioran, Roland Barthes, and William Gass, to whom she also was drawn. She even liked Newman's pipe tobacco, and once told me she was a little bit in love with him. Why not, I thought. Most of our friends, men and women, were at least a little bit in love with Charlie, and one reason Susan liked coming up to visit us and stay for a while in July was that he was always there. In 1984, when *Salmagundi* brought out a special issue devoted to his monograph *The Post-Modern Aura*, Susan thought it was one of the best things we had ever published, and she told him so. Like Susan, Charlie wanted more than anything else to be a novelist, a great novelist, though his best work was a long essayistic piece of cultural criticism. When he told her he'd been working for at least a decade on a very long novel, she assured him he'd finish it eventually, and he believed her.

Twenty years later, when his novel was still unfinished, and he was drinking a lot, Susan lost patience with him, and chastised me for being an enabler, for helping him to feel still relevant and hiring him year after year at the Summer Writers Institute. Why don't you tell him that he's wasting his talent, that there comes a time when a writer just has to tell himself the truth? It counted for very little with Susan that Charlie was one of my best friends. In the past, he had rented a summer house in Saratoga Springs in order to be with us, to have dinner with our kids each night, and to go with our family to New York City ballet performances several nights each week at the Performing Arts Center.

In addition, as I reminded Susan on several occasions, I had read more than eight hundred pages of Charlie's mammoth novel-in-progress, and thought many passages, even whole chapters, worthy of Robert Musil or Hermann Broch, though disjointed and in need of further revision. In the late '90s, when he read excerpts to audiences at the Summer Writers Institute, everyone present thought he was creating a work of wit and originality. A feral, comic Central European epic, inspired by *The Man Without Qualities*. Marilynne Robinson, Russell Banks, and others on our faculty thought it the single best presentation they'd heard in a summer of more than thirty readings. Though Susan was skeptical about a manuscript that had taken so long to come together, and was already ridiculously oversized, she continued to find Charlie good company and irresistibly dashing. You're sure that Peg doesn't enjoy having him around even more than you do? Susan asked. "Thanks for looking out for me," I would say when she intimated that maybe I should be worried, though this was Susan's way of playfully injecting dramatic intensity into a marital setting—mine—that seemed to her improbably stable and undramatic.

When Charlie became ill in 2004 Susan spoke of this as "tragic," and she was right. Presumably he would never bring his book to completion, and though I assured her there was already something like a finished draft, she didn't think he had been in any shape to make satisfactory revisions in such a work. Susan herself was ill that year—her final illness—and though we thought to press Charlie's manuscript on her, we knew that was a poor idea, and never mentioned the possibility either to her or to him. As it happened, Charlie made a brief comeback late in 2004, and we saw him once in late December, just before Susan died on the twenty-eighth of that month. Inevitable that I should wonder, again and again, what Susan would have made of the manuscript I had on my desk, in four bright blue folders. Two years later, Peg and I each delivered tributes to Charlie in St. Louis at a Washington University Memorial meeting organized by William Gass. It occurred to us that

Susan would have wanted to be there speaking of Charlie. In fact, she might well have selected as her theme the one I chose for a memoiristic essay on Charlie a few years later, "On Beauty." Would she have begun her remarks with something like the opening line of my essay: "The most beautiful man I ever knew was Charles Newman"? An idle question, perhaps. She was, as I note of her in that essay on Charlie, "an insatiable beauty lover," and often she allowed herself to swoon—playfully, openly, generously, girlishly—at the mere sight of Charles Newman as he entered an auditorium or took a chair at the dining table in our Saratoga Springs home. A 2002 email letter from Susan, responding to something I'd written her about Charlie's novel-in-progress, asks if he's "still beautiful."

Charlie left his money—a substantial sum—to the Chamber Music Society of Lincoln Center. Possibly a decision he made one day when he was drunk or disoriented on his way to a lawyer's meeting he had scheduled months earlier. At the time of his death he was estranged from just about everyone in his family who had been involved with us in several futile attempts to stage interventions to save him from his drinking. Susan regarded those efforts as hopeless, and thought Charlie was a man determined not to do what might have saved him. A complicated assessment in that he continued, right up to his death in March 2006, to hunger for the sharp pleasures he had always sought. Hunger for women especially. I knew I could entertain Susan by telling her stories about his exploits, his marriages, his infidelities, his way of making women feel that they inspired in him irrepressible desires. You don't think, do you, Susan once asked, that he aspires to your situation, and clings to you because he feels you have the secret to something he doesn't have? Occasionally Charlie did profess to be looking for "the one woman" who would turn things around for him, and when he was sixty, he spoke of wanting to have a child with his last wife, Edyth, to whom he was relentlessly unfaithful. Susan laughed when she heard him speak of wanting a child, but later that night, when we accompanied her back to her apartment, she said she felt bad about laughing. Charlie Newman was a man who really didn't know what he wanted, she said.

4 · AUTHORITY FIGURE

OVER the years, I wondered what Susan would think of an essay or review I published. Only rarely did she tell me, mainly when she disapproved. She wrote to me in 1966, after I published a review of *Against Interpretation* in the third issue of *Salmagundi*. In hindsight, I cannot explain why I wrote that for all their merits, there was nothing charming in her early essays. Like other young New York intellectuals, I was conducting my education in public, and I knew at once Susan had been overly generous when she wrote: "I did read your essay on my book of essays, of course. I'm afraid I don't enjoy reading about myself, but I will concede that, with your essay, the experience was less painful than I anticipated." That Susan continued to write to me now and then after I sent her my inadequate review says more about her capacity for forgiveness than about the few genuinely prescient things I said about her, at a time when we hadn't met, and she was spending a good deal of time in Europe.

My own letters to Sontag in the years before we became friends contained invitations of one sort or another. Would she write a review for *Salmagundi* magazine, or perhaps respond to an article we'd just published by Stanley Kauffmann (on Antonioni's film *Blow-Up*), or to one of the essays we'd been bring-

ing out by Fredric Jameson on Frankfurt School thinkers like
Walter Benjamin and T. W. Adorno? Good reason for me to be
often apologizing in those letters for trying so persistently to
lure her to write for us. "Sorry to be bombarding you with
notes," I wrote in a 1967 letter—the sort of apology I directed
more than occasionally at other writers—among them, Christopher Lasch, Martin Jay, Roger Shattuck, William H. Gass, Jed
Perl—who soon wrote regularly for us.

Our first meeting was at Skidmore College in 1975, when
she took the train upstate from New York to sit for a public
interview with me and a friend, Maxine Bernstein. Susan
seemed relaxed and was clearly delighted that the text of the
interview would appear in the tenth anniversary issue of
Salmagundi. Already she'd sent us a quote to use in ads, and she
was especially curious about my inordinate commitment to
the work of her former husband, Philip Rieff. In 1972, we'd
published a special issue, "Psychological Man: Approaches to
an Emergent Social Type" that featured a book-length essay by
Rieff. "You know," she wrote soon after, "it's strange that someone who thinks so highly of my work would also be attracted
to Philip's."

Was this, in fact, so strange? At the time, I couldn't think
why it would be. Sontag and Rieff were, to be sure, very different kinds of writers, and their politics could not have been
more different. Yet both had a way of putting into circulation
ideas that others would take up and develop. From our first
hours together in Saratoga Springs, Susan made it clear that
one big reason she looked forward to our meeting was my
interaction with Rieff. He's funny, isn't he? she would ask. You
couldn't make him up. A parody of something. A self-parody.
Those vests. Those hats. Those shoes.

Susan did not often seem competitive in the way others say

she was, but I had no doubt that her initial willingness to draw close to me, and to my magazine, had much to do with Rieff. With her sense that Rieff had managed to insinuate himself into my good graces and that, in turn, I had managed to persuade thinkers like Norman O. Brown, Christopher Lasch, and George Steiner to write about him. Over the next thirty years Susan would often say that Peg and I were her only friends who really knew Rieff, even though she understood we rarely saw him, and that our relationship with him never rose to the level of a genuine friendship. While I taught Rieff's *The Triumph of the Therapeutic* in my graduate courses at The New School for Social Research, and occasionally published his essays in *Salmagundi*, he was never a part of my life in the way Susan was. On the singular occasion when we spent time together— he had come for two weeks to Skidmore College to team teach with me and a colleague, Robert Orrill, a one-month course called "From Freud to Rieff: Toward A Theory of Culture"— we spoke more or less entirely of books and ideas, and I failed to draw Rieff out on anything personal. Never did he allude to his son, David, or to David's life with Susan.

On the other hand, Susan was more than willing to speak of Rieff, either with a smile or a sneer. At the 1974 public interview, I took a chance and asked her to respond to a passage from Rieff's *The Triumph of the Therapeutic,* where he might well have been referring to Susan. Among intellectuals, Rieff argued, there had lately been "a general shifting of sides," so that many had "gone over to the enemy" and "become spokesmen for what Freud called the instinctual mass."

"Would you say," I asked Susan, "that in attempting to legitimize 'an easier relation between popular culture and the elite culture' you had, in effect, 'gone over to the enemy'"?

Susan laughed at the question, and went on to speak of the distinction as "a vulgar one."

"Vulgar in what sense?"

"The distinction," she said, "suggests a contempt for the instincts, a facile pessimism about people, and a lack of passion for the arts." She disliked terms like "cultural elites" because they were "virtually unusable" and reflected a failure to acknowledge what was obvious in the arts. Did not Rieff understand that high culture had assimilated shards of low culture in beneficial ways, and that, by the 1960s, the popular arts, notably film and rock music, had taken up the abrasive themes and some of the "difficult" techniques (like collage) that had hitherto been the fare of a restricted cultural elite? If Rieff had important observations about other matters, it was nonetheless clear he had little understanding of modernism and of the processes that had been going on at least since Baudelaire. It was also clear Susan could speak of such matters with what she called "high seriousness," unapologetic about having recourse to an old-fashioned term with a decidedly Arnoldian flavor. Her willingness to promote high seriousness always seemed essential to Susan's importance, her refusal ever to capitulate to someone else's idea of what was or was not suitable for a proponent of the avant-garde.

As for Rieff, she was rarely less than scathing about his use of "Toryish labels," his "middlebrow" tendencies, and his employment of "self-congratulatory terms" for "diagnoses of cultural sickness." When I put to her a question about Rieff's anatomy of the contemporary university in his *Fellow Teachers*, which he had addressed to me and Robert Orrill, she responded in much the same way, by mocking his "empty definitions of great teacher and great student." Everything in Rieff's book seemed to her "grossly inadequate," his conception of authority "truculent" and an expression of "wishful thinking."

However much I disagreed with aspects of Susan's attack on Rieff, I was moved not only by the pointed ferocity of her critique , but by the fact that she had come to our interview fully prepared to speak of his work. Moved, moreover, by her eloquence. Never any doubt that Susan was as brilliant on her feet as on the page, that she would always be, as she proved again and again, to be the smartest person in the room. Though she was by no means an authority on the history of education, or on competing philosophic conceptions of authority, she spoke of these issues comfortably and fluently, as beautifully as she spoke of artists and artworks to which she had devoted lengthy essays. The following excerpts from the interview—two modest passages responding to Rieff—were taken down directly from the unedited transcript:

When in Western intellectual history did the college teacher have an absolute and irreducible authority'? Even in the great ages of faith, which one might suppose well-stocked with models for the pedagogue as dictator, a closer look discloses a reassuring ferment of dissent, of heterodoxy, of questioning what was "already known." Fiat cannot restore to the office of the teacher (now irrevocably secular, transmitting a plurality of "traditions") an absolute authority which both the teacher and what is being taught do not have—if they ever did.

Even in the Maoist conception of the relation between leaders and masses, the authority of the Great Teacher does not derive, tautologically, from his authority, but from his wisdom—a much advertised part of which consists in overturning "what is already known." Though Rieff's notion of the teacher has more in common with the Maoist pedagogic conception than with the main tradition of Western activity and high culture which he thinks he's defending—against barbarous students—it is formulated in a fashion more dismissive of independence of thought than Maoism.

Susan thought well enough of her performance in this interview not only to have it featured in the *Salmagundi* issue for which it had been intended, but also to include it in *The Susan Sontag Reader* (1982) that she assembled for publication some years later. In many ways, I continue to believe our long friendship, and her participation in many symposia and public events sponsored by the magazine, had much to do, at least initially, with my odd connection to Rieff and his work. I won't even try to get to the bottom of that intimation, and refuse to reduce the origins of our friendship to sheer competiveness or spite on Susan's part. That she delighted in the opportunity we had provided to explain her hostility to Rieff and his work was clear. But the interview also gave Susan a chance to set the record straight on several other fronts.

Over the years we often talked with one another about the idea of authority, and though I never told her that she was for me an improbable authority figure, she surely knew it was so. Why improbable? For one thing, because she allowed me to know her very well, and even to see her at her worst, her most vulnerable, her least appealing. How, I wondered, could such a person continue to be an authority figure? What could the term mean when applied to Susan? How would a more or less sane person like myself continue to regard as an exemplar someone who often behaved badly and occasionally subjected her friend to humiliation?

It's complicated, I would tell myself, and continued to intone those words even when, not very long ago, I wrote a long essay on authority and attempted to explain my peculiar relationship to someone I loved and sometimes feared and disliked. That Rieff had written a great deal on authority over the years was another source of inspiration for thinking about the subject, and though Rieff could never have been an authority figure for me—he was too pompous, remote, and politically conservative—I knew that Susan was herself susceptible to the lure of authority figures. I knew it because now and then she spoke of these individuals with a veneration that was palpable, and because a number of her greatest essays are devoted to thinkers she regarded as her masters: Roland Barthes, Walter Benjamin, Elias Canetti, and others. Though she never quite said anything to match Canetti's words on his willing subordination to the Viennese satirist Karl Kraus, she did find Canetti's willing subordination thrilling, as she told me more than once, although she found the extremity of his attachment appalling.

Consider Canetti's pronouncement: "For at that time, I truly experienced what it means to live in a dictatorship. I was its voluntary, its devoted, its passionate and enthusiastic follower. Any foe of Karl Kraus's was a corrupt, an immoral creature." In fact, Canetti explained:

> After you heard ten or twelve lectures by Karl
> Kraus, after you read his journal *Die Fackel* for a year
> or two, the first thing to happen was a general shrink-
> age of the desire to do your own judging. There was
> an invasion of powerful and relentless decisions that
> did not brook the slightest doubt. Once something was

decided by this supreme authority, it was considered settled; people would have regarded it as impudent to even test it for themselves.[33]

These were not the words of an adolescent. Canetti was a youthful but mature infatuate. He understood that what he experienced was temporary, though his obsession lasted for some years, and he never came to regret it. He never ceased to believe, as he wrote, that "it is important to look up to a model who has a rich, turbulent, unmistakable world, a world that he has smelled for himself, seen for himself, heard for himself, felt for himself, devised for himself . . . I cannot imagine a writer," Canetti continued, "who was not controlled and paralyzed by someone else's authenticity at an early age," until eventually "his [own] concealed powers begin to stir." Canetti knew there were dangers in such adulation, "something fateful about models who reach down into this darkness, cutting off one's breath." But there was even greater danger, he argued, in weak models, "who practice bribery" and "make one think that one's own world already exists merely because one bows to them in humility. One ultimately lives by their grace as a well-trained animal and is content with delicacies from their hand."[34]

Susan was by no means a "well-trained animal." She longed to be in the company of those with rich and turbulent worlds of their own. Her masters were thinkers to whom she was disposed, unambivalently, to pay homage. She studied them, and absorbed them, and promoted them. She measured her own ambitions and achievements against theirs. Her essays on the selected masters are frankly devotional, at once intimate and impersonal. They do not reek of a slavish subordination but supply evidence of a willing suspension of self in the approach to an imposing consciousness. Nowhere else in her work is she so earnest in what she called her "willingness to serve." She wished, after all, to identify completely with the ardor, the intellectual intensity, of those she admired, and she appropriated their most bracing ideas with the hunger of one who needed them to breathe. You had only to be in her presence for a short while to see that she understood what Stendhal intended when he said his soul was a "fire that consumes itself when it is not ablaze."[35]

In truth, I am not such a person. Though I pass for "intense" in the standard academic circles where caution, indifference, and groupthink usually prevail, Susan really was the embodiment of an ardor I could never match. Like her, I have never stopped myself from saying what was on my mind merely to make things easy for myself or to pander to some powerful faction. But I am, by temperament, more forgiving and tolerant than Susan, and her authority always was attractive and forbidding to me. Hers was not the authority of an impeccably decent or lovely person who embodied the wisdom of temperance, balance, unimpeachable good nature. No compulsory sweetness, nothing benign in Susan, no gentle will to exemplify the exemplary. No sense in my feeling for her that she would be good for me, that she would make me a better person than I was.

Principally, I felt in my sense of Susan as an authority figure that I must labor to be worthy of the interest she took in me. I'll never forget the times she offered her approval of something I had written, though I knew I could not be as implacable in my judgment as she was, nor did I wish to be. At times, in her presence, I felt small and supposed that it was the result of her desire to cast doubt on my more modest ambitions and to belittle my inveterate habits of courtesy and moderation.

When I called her on some casual disparagement she had directed at me, she reacted with astonishment. Occasionally, when she unwittingly conveyed her sense of the unbridgeable gap that separated us, I could only laugh and leave her wondering at what she had said that could be so funny.

Our differences were not always laughing matters. In a November 1978 letter Susan registers what she calls "a strenuous complaint" about an essay I had written for the *Times Literary Supplement* at a time when I was writing often for that publication. My subject was the quarterly magazine *Modern Occasions*, whose editor, Philip Rahv, a founding editor of *Partisan Review*, had resigned in protest against the direction the magazine had lately taken. That direction had much to do with *Partisan Review*'s publication of essays on rock music, pornography, and other such subjects by people like Richard Poirier, Leslie Fiedler, and Susan. "Unconscionable," Susan fumed, that I would suggest she had "anything to do with, or shared any views with Leslie Fiedler," and "astonished that you echoed Rahv's misreading and hostile judgment." In truth, I had no wish to disparage such writers or the subjects they chose to write about. I published work by Susan in *Salmagundi* and essays by Fiedler as well as a long interview with Poirier, and I wrote for *Harper's* and other magazines my own essays extolling the virtues of such writers. Fortunately, soon after Susan sent her furious letter, we spent a long evening together in Manhattan, and though she never quite accepted that it was not so very terrible to be associated with Leslie Fiedler, she agreed that in what I wrote there was no "hostile judgment of her work."

Another instance, among many I might cite, occurred in 2001: Lewis Lapham of *Harper's* had invited me to write a series of essays that would make the case for writers—mainly foreign writers—who deserved to be better known in the United States. One of the first essays I wrote for the series focused on the Italian novelist and woman of letters Natalia Ginzburg. At dinner one night with Susan and several other writers, she recommended my Ginzburg essay to her friend and translator, Paolo di Leonardo, and went on to say how pleased she was that I was writing for the large *Harper*'s readership, most of whom would not, alas, appreciate what they were getting in those highly "sophisticated" essays. Of course, Susan continued, she would never write for a mid-cult magazine like *Harper's*, though she was especially pleased that I was appearing frequently in those pages.

Was this hilarious? I thought it was, and though I merely laughed when the words issued from Susan's lips, I thought it best not to explain what was "so funny" about her charming effort to "celebrate" what I was doing. Maybe equally hilarious, when I think about it, is that Susan never entirely ceased to be an authority figure for me. Always I struggled with the sense that the development of my own powers required an exertion not easy to make, that Susan existed somehow as a standing affront to what felt right and natural and in keeping with my own disposition. To reconcile the tension informing my sense of vocation would have required that I thoroughly dispense with, or yield to, the voice of authority—Susan's voice—driving me on and, in some degree, blocking my way to self-approval.

Susan was often attracted to the transgressive. She not only tolerated but craved, in the domains of art and thought, what Rieff called "the instabilities that are the modern condition."[36] Though we were both drawn to modernism, Susan's appetite for what Lionel Trilling called "spiritual militancy" went deeper than mine. I tended to mistrust militancy rather more than she did, and I found comfort in homelier virtues—moderation and generosity—that Susan could rarely bring herself to applaud or embrace.

Susan was volatile and unpredictable. A person not only of moods and ambivalences but of surprising turns and contradictions. Much though I sought to find a way to detach myself from the species of devotion she inspired—and was more than once tempted to escape the discomfort she caused—I stayed with her, even felt from time to time her odd dependence on me and others whose loyalty she sought. When she phoned me in Saratoga Springs one morning and asked if Peg and I might not drive to New York City "tomorrow" to "support" her at her "graduation" from a "smoke-enders" course, I thought yes, perfectly right: Susan wants us to bear witness to a protocol both meaningful and preposterous. She wants us to laugh about the strangeness of the ceremony and to remember that she could stand and declare herself, in a room full of strangers and fellow sinners, as one who had been a smoker and had managed to "cure" herself, and was improbably proud to say so. To a degree that was not easy to fathom, Susan required, craved, some semblance of fellow-feeling from a handful of people who found her not merely fascinating but by turns irresistible and impossible. She was, for all her apparent conviviality and the access she had to the best and liveliest minds of her generation, a lonely person who needed loyal friends who could be counted on to love her in spite of what she routinely put them through. That sense of her neediness sustained me in times when she was at her imperious worst and never diminished that other sense of her as a commanding and exemplary presence.

5 · "TURN OF THE CULTURAL WHEEL"

EXEMPLARY? You thought her exemplary? How ever can that be? my friends would ask. Most often my explanations would fail to convince and I would try again to get to the bottom of Susan, to savor again her signal virtues. In "Elias Canetti," an essay in *Granta* in 1982, she wrote of aphoristic thinking that it is "informal, unsociable, adversarial, proudly selfish." Susan liked to think not only of her writing but of herself in those terms, though she was not invariably adversarial or fatally selfish. She wanted things her way but she was often not only sociable but gregarious. She craved company and conversation. She hated our lengthy Manhattan dinners to come to an end. She was—apologies for the cliché—a terrific listener. Never once at any social occasion did I hear her lecture or insist on holding the floor. Despite her inclination to be overbearing, her investment in sweeping dicta and generalizations, she longed for comrades who would help her to resist verdicts and resolutions.

Is it impossible that a person who often issued commands and resolutions should have wished not always to be that person? Susan felt the pull, the allure, of ideas, images, beautiful objects, attractive faces and bodies. In her best writing she darts

Robert Boyers with Susan Sontag in 1974 at Skidmore College, where he interviewed her for *Salmagundi*.

Robert Boyers and Lionel Trilling at Skidmore College, 1973.

Tom Lewis, Robert Boyers, and Peg Boyers, *Salmagundi* editorial staff, at the magazine offices, Skidmore College, 1979.

Charles Newman and Susan Sontag at the New York State Summer Writers
Institute, Skidmore College, 1998.

Tom Lewis, Susan Sontag, and Gary Indiana at the *Salmagundi* "Kitsch
Conference," Skidmore College, 1989.

Irving Howe (*center*) with other participants at the *Salmagundi* "Kitsch Conference," Skidmore College, 1989.

Robert Boyers and Susan Sontag at the New York State Summer Writers Institute,
Skidmore College, 1992.

Susan Sontag at the Lyrical Ballad Bookstore, Saratoga Springs, 1994.

David Rieff and Susan Sontag at the New York State Summer Writers Institute, Skidmore College, 1996.

Susan Sontag and Gabriel Boyers, Saratoga Springs, 2001.

Susan Sontag, Robert Boyers, and Nadine Gordimer at the International Pen Conference, New York City, 1986. Photograph by Miriam Berkeley.

vertiginously from one striking observation to another, the argumentation definite but fragmented, the speaker collecting thoughts with a restless, resistless intensity, always poised to move on to another insight just as striking. This vigor was as much a feature of her table talk as of her characteristic writing. She loved and feared contradiction in more or less equal measure. She wanted to be definite and yet to entertain, with full attentiveness, everything that undercut even her deepest instincts. Deeply drawn to photographs, she wrote *On Photography*, a great book that exhibited, above all, what one writer called the "moral disquiet" occasioned by her own attraction. Inclined to write about her subject with a disciplined aesthetic refinement, she found herself focusing on the "aggression," "mercilessness," "appropriativeness," and even the transgressiveness of photography. Always poised to resist efforts to politicize art or to reduce art to morality, she yet found herself dwelling on what she called "the distortions by which consumerism threatens our world." To say that hers was a voracious and restless intelligence is to say not nearly enough.

The happiest three days of my professional life covered a long weekend in 1989 when two dozen writers and intellectuals sat around an enormous conference table at Skidmore College, speaking with one another for fifteen hours about kitsch. Not one of those we invited to this intimate conference—conducted without an audience—doubted the subject might prove interesting, although others would surely think the topic marginal, even a waste of time. Kitsch was a subject once much talked about in New York intellectual circles, inspired in no small measure by a famous 1939 essay, "Avant-Garde and Kitsch," by the art critic Clement Greenberg.[37] What was controversial in Greenberg's essay seemed to me, to Sontag, and to others as compelling in the present as it had seemed to its first readers decades earlier. Though none of us quite believed that "the avant-garde forms the only living culture we now have," or that there was any longer a "general agreement . . . as to what is good art and what bad," most of us did worry about the way that "spurious" values had obscured our understanding of the relationship between art and society, and we wondered whether it was essential to distinguish between "those values only to be found in art and the values which can be found elsewhere." Was it true that the "kitsch" formulas, devised to appeal to people "hungry" for "diversion" but resistant to genuinely demanding works of art, had fatally compromised our capacity to respond to what was best in our culture?

Others in the New York intellectual community had written on related matters, most notably Dwight MacDonald in his polemic "Masscult and Midcult." Several leading writers and thinkers, including Hermann Broch and Harold Rosenberg, wrote important essays on kitsch, and in 1986 the historian Saul Friedländer brought out a deeply unsettling book called *Reflections of Nazism: An Essay on Kitsch and Death.* Susan admired the book as much as I did, and when Friedländer agreed to participate in the conference we were planning, I imagined that we might well open up a new way to think about culture and politics.

Also important, for our purposes, was that Susan had come to fame in 1965 with "Notes on 'Camp,'" which had not ceased to inspire and provoke. Though an enormous gap separated kitsch from camp, and both of those from masscult and midcult, it seemed impossible to think seriously about any one of these concepts without considering the others. When I invited Susan to participate, she agreed at once, and helped me assemble a dossier of readings that all participants would be assigned. Friedländer's would be the most imposing of the texts, and Susan recommended that he be asked to lead off the conference with opening remarks, after which we'd have the kind of free-for-all that Susan loved at *Salmagundi* magazine conferences.

Susan hadn't met most of the participants, including my colleagues in the Skidmore College English Department. Among the others were the critics Irving Howe and Stanley Kauffmann, the philosophers Robert Nozick and Berel Lang, the political theorist Yaron Ezrahi, and the artist, writer, and cultural critic Gary Indiana. Some longstanding antipathies were set aside, at least provisionally. Everyone resided in the same college facility, taking meals together over three days. Opportunities for posturing and grandstanding were resisted. Everyone was free to venture and risk.

No question that in this lively and various assemblage, Sontag was the speaker everyone wanted most to hear from. Content to be, in every way, the ideal participant. Eager, inquisitive, courteous, occasionally contentious but never brutal. Not a diva but, like everyone else at the table, a humble worker, driven by a desire to understand kitsch in a way it had never quite been understood before, and to discover what made the idea of kitsch oddly compelling. Susan was by turns enthusiastic and skeptical, circling her prey, not to pin or anesthetize it but to keep it very much in motion, an idea, a phenomenon that might continue to seem puzzling and curious, if also appalling or revolting.

One reason—surely the primary reason—those days were the happiest of my professional life was that Susan was clearly very happy. She was in her element, not surrounded by a roomful of old friends but by new friends. Friends, at least for three days. Clearly challenged and pushed by the opinions of others and yet stirred to be her best self. Generosity of spirit obvious even when Susan disagreed or corrected. A beneficent accent now and then discernible in her essays, though rarely so poignant.

A brief passage from the edited transcript of the conference—taken from the Spring 1990 *Salmagundi* special issue on kitsch—suggests what we were up to on those memorable days of amiable contention. The following exchange was inspired by the reading of Rupert Brooke's famous World War I poem, "The Soldier," which several speakers thought a plausible example of kitsch.

> If I should die, think only this of me:
> That there's some corner of a foreign field
> That is forever England. There shall be
> In that rich earth a richer dust concealed;
> A dust whom England bore, shaped, made aware,
> Gave, once, her flowers to love, her ways to roam;
> A body of England's, breathing English air,
> Washed by the rivers, blest by suns of home.
>
> And think, this heart, all evil shed away,
> A pulse in the eternal mind, no less
> Gives somewhere back the thoughts by England given;
> Her sights and sounds; dreams happy as her day;
> And laughter, learnt of friends; and gentleness,
> In hearts at peace, under an English heaven.

Charles Molesworth: The poem relies, for its chief sentiment, on a form of nationalism, which is very much an ideology used by others, historically, to shackle. Brooke believes in the myth of a kind of transcendent-sentimental nationalism which is very near the heart of kitsch.

Susan Kress: It seems to me that one can argue that the poet himself is innocent but that his sources are not.

Sidra Ezrahi: As Paul Fussell points out, the ironizing voice entered the writing of war poetry in WW I and has since become accepted as the prevailing mode in war literature worthy of our attention. . . . I think we have come to a point where we read most texts expressing nationalistic sentiments as kitsch. There's not much help for that.

Susan Sontag: I'm very unsusceptible to nationalist sentiments. But I don't consider them to be as evil as many people here think they are. Some great poetry was written in Hungary and Poland in the 19th and early 20th centuries by poets who were striving to create and sustain national identity. . . . And I must say I don't feel it's kitsch, maybe simply because those sentiments always seem very beautiful when voiced by representatives of people who don't have power. Brooke is writing about an England which was—even in his day—the most powerful country in the world. Sentiments like those voiced in America today seem very different than if they are voiced in, say, Poland. I think there's a context even for "sentimental nationalism." You can't help making a judgment about power as well as feeling when you think about these matters.

Charles Molesworth: I didn't mean to say that kitsch is always nationalistic or that nationalism is always kitsch . . . but I've also seen the uses to which nationalistic feelings have been put.

Susan Sontag: I see something entirely different in the Brooke poem. Brooke was one of the handsomest men on the planet; everyone who met him said his beauty was overpowering. And I think there is a narcissism in this poem (and in a lot of his work) which affects the nationalism. But aside from that, as Stanley [Kauffmann] said, this is a bad poem, not kitsch. Kitsch is generally pretentious.[38]

Although there is much to argue about even in these compact passages, I want to convey Susan's pleasure in conversation for its own sake. Conversation where there is no end game or determinate purpose. Though Susan could be—often was—a polemicist arguing a position or putting away an opponent, she was also much of the time "merely" an appreciator, an intellectual lover, sharing a thought, trying out an idea, listening and responding.

This aspect of Susan's nature—call it generosity—is reflected as well in her willingness to change her mind, to rethink and revise. Some of her reversals were notorious, as in 1982, at a rally in support of Poland's Solidarity Movement at the Town Hall in Manhattan, when she corrected what she took to be her own naïve political view of the left with the public statement that included the words "Communism is fascism with a human face."[39]

The kind of statement that cost her many friends and supporters. And brave too was her reversal, in her second book on photography, *Regarding the Pain of Others*, where she wrote: "As much as they create sympathy . . . photographs shrivel sympathy. Is this true? I thought it was when I wrote it in *On Photography*. I'm not so sure now."

The most important reversal Susan ever made occurred about a decade after she first won fame in the 1960s. We talked about this reversal in our first interview session, in 1974, and spoke of it again, more insistently, when her greatest essay, "Fascinating Fascism," first appeared in the *New York Review of Books* in 1975. The focus was the German filmmaker Leni Riefensthal, whom it had once seemed possible to make a case for as a great director, though she made her films at the behest of Adolf Hitler. In fact, Sontag argued, she had directed films "whose very conception negates the possibility of the filmmaker's having an aesthetic conception independent of propaganda."

There are so many sly and seductive observations in Sontag's essay—about fascism and fascist aesthetics, about the relationship of sex to sadomasochism, about beauty and the quotidian—that it seems impossible to overstate its importance. What impressed me most was Susan's willingness to argue that sophisticated people in liberal societies—people like herself—are susceptible to "cycles of taste" which can enable them to "distill out the controversy" otherwise certain to be generated by particular works of art. In so doing, they may conceal from themselves what is at stake in works—like Riefensthal's—they feel called upon to celebrate or admire and, in effect, to ratify their own advanced taste. In this way, Riefensthal's films may be reduced only to their "aesthetic" merits, in a process Susan herself had found compelling and eminently effective when she was writing her first essays. "But the judgments of taste themselves seem less innocent," she wrote: "Art that seemed eminently worth defending ten years ago, as a minority or adversary taste, no longer seems defensible today, because the ethical and cultural issues it raises have become serious, even dangerous, in a way they were not then. The hard truth," Susan explained, "is that what may be acceptable in elite culture may not be acceptable in mass culture, that tastes which pose only innocuous ethical issues as the property of a minority become corrupting when they become more established. Taste is context, and the context has changed."

In writing "Fascinating Fascism," Susan opened herself to enormous controversy. Even those of us who thought she had done what seemed brave and essential were bound to entertain misgivings. In my case, the misgivings had much to do with the question of context. To be sure, I felt, "taste is context," just as she argued. But what had been for Susan the tipping point at which the ethical issues alluded to had suddenly come to seem dangerous? Was there not always danger in the tendency to aestheticize? And wasn't that danger cited and anatomized in the writings of others long before she wrote her essay? What made the moment Susan chose for a revaluation of "context" the right and inevitable moment?

We talked about similar questions frequently in the years that followed, and they played an important role in the conversations about kitsch that both of us found so stirring. But Susan's willingness to align herself with what she referred to as "elite" culture and to step decisively away from any association with "mass culture" marked a significant departure, and surely confused and discomfited many of those who had earlier thought her an unambivalent, undivided spokesperson for whatever seemed "adversarial" and "dangerous." When I told her that I'd never imagined she would come around to a view of the emergent "adversary culture" earlier propounded by Lionel Trilling in "The Fate of Pleasure," she laughed and reminded me that anything is possible "with the turn of the cultural wheel."[40]

6 · THE THERAPEUTIC

S
USAN occasionally spoke of her most recent encounters with a "shrink." That she had need of one was a given, though by her own estimation, she was not apt to rid herself of conflicts and stresses that could be overmastering. Did she think well of her shrink? Admire him? "Why would I need to admire him?" Susan would ask. Which would lead us to compare notes. Though I had little experience as a patient, never quite believing I needed therapy, my closest friend for a decade was the psychoanalyst Leslie H. Farber, author of *The Ways of The Will*, whose work Susan read with some interest, admiring especially his essay "Lying On The Couch," which I had published in a special issue of *Salmagundi* in 1974. Les had fixed me up with a psychoanalyst at one point in the early 1970s when my first wife and I were divorcing and I was preparing to marry Peg. When I told Susan about that weird, abortive, short-lived episode, she laughed and agreed that I was not a suitable candidate for therapy. Neither did she think that Les, who died in April 1981, would have been a suitable therapist for her. "There's something about him," she told me, thinking it best not to go further. Though I invited her to the memorial I organized for Les in Manhattan shortly after his death, she was traveling at the time, but expressed surprise that the speakers I assembled with the help of Les's widow, Anne

Farber, included not only writers like Robert Jay Lifton, but also a number of Les's former patients.

I was most inclined to think that Susan needed help when she acted out in ways that were destructive, especially when she erupted into the angry, resentful, self-important fury that wasn't her best or most characteristic self. On a night in the mid-1990s, after she had returned from one of her many trips to Sarajevo, she spoke to an audience at Skidmore College about the Bosnian war. She was doing beautifully until a young man asked a question, an articulate and lengthy question. "You sound," she said, "like someone who is terribly eager to impress everyone here with your own profound experience of the Bosnian conflict. But what, really, do you know? Don't be shy. I'm curious."

"I just wanted to ask," the young man said. "I've seen you here many times and I always like to hear you talk."

"But you're evading my question. I mean, you don't ask a long-winded question like that without wanting to impress everyone with how much you already know."

"Well," said the young man, seated six or seven rows back from the podium, "I have spent most of the last two years in Sarajevo, covering the war for a German newspaper. So, I'm not exactly without any experience of what's going on there."

"You see," said Susan. "That's what I'm getting at. There's a presumption there in what you say, as if spending time in a place is evidence somehow that you know what's important. Don't you think," she went on, "that you can spend time in a place and understand very little?"

"I do," he replied. "I do believe that, and that's why I wanted to hear what you would have to say."

"What I have to say," Susan said, as if she had been insulted or challenged, "is that while you've been doing what reporters do, and for all I know picking up this or that, I've met with all of the major players in Sarajevo, and received the key to the city. I don't think anyone has offered you the key to the city. Am I wrong?"

"No, you're not wrong," said the young man, "and thank you for your very helpful response to my question."

Later that evening Susan wanted to know who that young man was, and I told her that he had been a student of mine at Skidmore about a decade earlier, that he now lived in Berlin, and had spent time in Bosnia and written a very good first book. I said she would like him. "You don't think he was presumptuous and annoying," she asked? "Not at all," I said. "I thought he handled himself very well." And, I thought, keeping this to myself, you really do need right away to spend some more time with your shrink. The pompous, bullying, self-importance of that public display seemed to me a sure sign that Susan was in need of the kind of help I could not provide.

On another occasion a year or two later she phoned on a Friday morning in early spring to say that she wanted to come up to visit us for a weekend in Saratoga Springs with an old friend, a woman whom we'd met before and liked. Could I book two rooms for them in the college's Surrey Inn, and plan for us to dine together that night? Easy to arrange, I said, and about five hours later Peg and I were at the Surrey Inn to hand them the keys and get them into their rooms. Susan's friend went ahead with Peg, and left me outside with Susan to speak briefly about the weekend ahead. I handed her a bag of modest supplies for the room—granola bars, a few juice bottles, a bar of Lindt chocolate. Pleased, grateful. She knew I wouldn't mind her visiting without prior warning. "Why would we mind?" I asked—though we might well have been out of town, as we were two or three weekends each month. "But why don't you go up and settle in, and we can meet in an hour and go to dinner?"

"Perfect," she said, and then added: "I know you like my friend. But I wouldn't want you to think there's anything between us. You wouldn't think that, would you? That's why I asked you to book two rooms. I mean," Susan went on, "I can do better than that."

Not, I suppose, a sure sign that Susan was in sudden need of a therapist, but an indication that she was often insecure, neurotic. Had I been her therapist, and heard her tell me what she had told her friend Boyers, assuring him that she could do better than the companion she had chosen for a weekend in upstate New York, I'd have invited her to pursue her desire to share that confidence, and consider where the need for reassurance came from.

When I think of Susan's struggles, her more-than-intermittent psychological distress, her openness about her unhappiness, and her recourse to sessions with a shrink, I find it odd she never cared to talk about neurosis, never so much as alluded to Freud or to infantile disorders, projection, primary narcissism, or transference. Never felt tempted to talk with me about the psychological ideal of normality, a dubious notion, to be sure, yet one which now and then came up in our conversations without tempting Susan at all.

Though Susan's almost total lack of interest in issues central to the psychoanalytic tradition seemed striking, she was invested in so many other intellectual issues that I never gave this particular avoidance much thought. She had written but one single review on a psychological subject. But now, in the wake of Benjamin Moser's Pulitzer-prize-winning biography, *Sontag: Her Life and Work* (2019), it's hard not to go back to her avoidance and consider what it entails. Might have entailed.

After all, the most bizarre aspect of Moser's biography is his claim that Susan was the author of her husband Philip Rieff's four-hundred-page book, *Freud: The Mind of the Moralist*. So decisive is Moser's argument that throughout his biography he mentions he's quoting from Susan's work when he turns to the Freud book, and even includes her name as the author in the footnotes for *The Mind of the Moralist*. Astonishing, no? To suggest Susan could have written a major work—she didn't write it, of course—that clearly took many years to compose, though Susan was for many decades wholly uninterested in the subject of *her* book.

Moser's claims are based upon a few pieces of "evidence." The first is the testimony of friends who knew Susan at the time of her marriage to Rieff and remember her speaking of his original manuscript draft as "still a mess," which it was up to her to improve. In a letter to her mother, Susan reports that she was "in third gear now on the book—working about ten hours a day on it at least." A friend admonishes her not to "relinquish all rights on the Freud," which "would be a crime." Another friend contends that Susan was "willing to give up the book to get rid of him." Most decisively, as Moser writes, four decades later, "a package was delivered" to Susan containing a copy of *Freud: The Mind of the Moralist*, "inscribed to 'Susan, Love of my life, mother of my son, co-author of this book: forgive me. Please. Philip.'"

Impossible to declare what is or is not reliable in this account. In her wonderful *Sempre Susan: A Memoir of Susan Sontag* (2011), Sigrid Nunez notes Susan's penchant for exaggeration. Joan Acocella, who interviewed Sontag for the *New Yorker* in 2000, observes that "Susan was just very, very difficult, and she lied. She lied a lot."[41] No doubt Susan did speak to others of the work she did on the Freud book. She was a superbly gifted line editor,

and I have in my *Salmagundi* magazine files many pages of symposia transcripts expertly amended by Susan. But then no one
reading her own essays could possibly doubt that she was an
incisive reader and critic. If she worked ten hours a day on the
manuscript of *Freud*, she would surely have made it much better. Editors often have that effect on the articles and books they
work on. Though some writers like to pretend they would
never allow an editor to meddle with their work, a great many
others pay homage to the extraordinary labors of their editors.
But in doing so they do not suggest that their editors thereby
became the coauthors—or indeed the authors—of their books.

I have no reason to dispute the inscription Rieff is said to
have written. However, the inscription would seem to reflect
an impulse that had more to do with the moment in which it
was written, a time when Susan was dealing with a recurrence
of the cancer that had nearly killed her almost twenty-five
years earlier. Moser makes it clear that the treatments to which
Susan was subjected between 1998 and 2000 were harrowing,
and in the years when she was in treatment we saw that she was
severely weakened. When we walked together, even a short
distance, Susan would sometimes ask to hold my arm, which
she had never done before. She worried about falling on the
stairs leading to an auditorium or a guest house. In New York
everyone in our circle knew what Susan was going through,
and Rieff surely knew because by that time his long estrange-
ment from their son, David Rieff, had come to an end, as David
told us on several occasions. Though Philip Rieff was not a
generous person, the inscription would suggest he understood
what Susan then felt: that she might not survive this ordeal, and
he wished to reach out to her in the only way then possible: by
capitulating to her version of what had transpired in the writing of the book on Freud. Was Rieff "serious" in his use of the

word "co-author"? Perhaps. But the context is surely worth taking into account in the case of so extraordinary a claim. Also worth noting is that in the first edition Rieff thanks "my wife, Susan Rieff, who devoted herself unstintingly to this book." This acknowledgment Moser describes as a "grudging nod," and goes on to note that a friend of Susan's knew at once in reading those words that "he hates her," given his use of a name "she never in her whole life used." However, this dispute about Susan's married name has little, if anything, to do with the question of authorship.

Moser's claim goes far beyond the notion of coauthorship and reflects his belief that a work which began as a doctoral dissertation by Rieff, who then worked for an extended time, shaping it, amassing large quantities of notes and documentary materials, could somehow have ceased to be his work. That belief seems to me insupportable. In fact, it is almost as insupportable as the notion that Susan, in essentially authoring the book, had full command not only of all of Freud's works but also of the entire psychoanalytic tradition. No subsequent evidence of that mastery or investment is anywhere available in Susan's writing. Nor was it ever suggested in anything that she said in my presence, not in private interactions, not in three-day symposia when she spoke at length about a great many subjects.

The other "evidence" Moser supplies can be summed up in a single sentence. "It is hard," he writes, "to imagine [*Freud: The Mind of the Moralist*] could be the product of a mind that later produced such meager fruits." No doubt those of us who admired Rieff's work were surprised that he published few books in the later decades of his life. But his 1966 masterpiece, *The Triumph of the Therapeutic: Uses of Faith After Freud,* was at least as well received as his book on Freud, and seemed to many of us a far more original and provocative work. In the *New York Times Book Review* Robert Coles wrote: "Rieff takes up where Nietzsche left off," the writing "sharp, witty, passionate, and at all times strikingly aphoristic."[42] One reviewer described *The Triumph* as "a great, crotchety, ironic, cool book." Philip Rahv wrote in *Book Week* that *The Triumph* was "even more absorbing [than *Freud:The Mind of the Moralist*] because of its revolutionary implications in the spheres of morals and culture." Much the same response came from major thinkers like Alasdair MacIntyre and critics like Frederick C. Crews. *The Triumph of the Therapeutic* was no meager fruit but a work of enormous importance, and the brilliance of the writing, dense with scholarship, attests to Rieff's mastery in a book he wrote by himself. All by himself.

Rieff was an eccentric thinker, whose crotchets were by no means palatable to some readers. But the notion that he could not possibly have authored the *The Mind of the Moralist* is nothing short of misleading. Susan knew very well that we regarded *The Triumph* as a major work and that many of those who wrote for *Salmagundi* had much the same view, not only of *The Triumph* but of the far more eccentric work *Fellow Teachers*, which was praised in the highest terms by such reviewers as Frank Kermode, George Steiner, C. P. Snow, and Alasdair MacIntyre.

We have only to quote from Rieff's work to see that at his best he was both an original and a brilliant writer whose aphoristically exacting sentences set him apart from other scholars.

FROM *The Triumph of the Therapeutic*:

I doubt that Western men can be persuaded again to the Greek opinion that the secret of happiness is to have as few needs as possible. The philosophers of therapeutic deprivation are disposed to eat well.

Psychological man takes on the attitude of a scientist, with himself alone as the ultimate object of his science.

The best one can say for oneself in life is that one has not been taken in, even by that "normal psychosis," love.[43]

FROM *Fellow Teachers*:

It takes a certain genius to survive the deepest hurts. Freud favored asking less of people, most of whom are not moral geniuses nor any other kind.

Theorists are obliged to be the unwed fathers of their ideas.

Why should the therapeutic feel anything deeply when he can exhibit his sensibilities?

Experience is a swindle; the experienced know that much.[44]

Rieff wrote a great many first-rate essays, including introductions to the ten-volume edition of Freud's papers. His 1980 *Salmagundi* essay on Oscar Wilde, "The Impossible Culture," was so extraordinarily original that Susan spoke of it as "surprisingly good" and added that she hadn't realized he "was still sending" us new work. The several posthumous books issued one after another following his death in 2011 were heavier, more relentlessly theoretical, than the books and essays published during his lifetime, but they were hardly "meager."

Susan didn't need to be the author of Rieff's book on Freud. However much she reviled him and hated what he was as a husband, she knew that he was a great deal more than a "meager" writer. She had reasons for wanting Rieff to appear awful and exploitative, as in many respects he surely was. But there is no good reason for Susan's biographer to make her the author of a book she didn't write.

7 · TO TEACH OR NOT TO TEACH

USAN didn't aspire to be a teacher. Though she taught—very infrequently—at several universities, she never saw teaching as a vocation. When I erupted, now and then, with an anecdote about a particularly impressive student in one of my classes, she would say, "Impressive?" or "I'm surprised you're still excited about them after so many years." Once I gave her a term paper focused on her work by a graduate student enrolled in my Cultural Criticism seminar at The New School and asked if she agreed that it was publishable. "It's easy," Susan said on the phone a few days later, "to be overly impressed by a merely intelligent paper when you've been reading the kinds of things you have to read, even in a graduate class." "Wouldn't you like to mentor such a student," I asked. "I don't think so," Susan replied.

The word "mentor" can imply different relationships. I don't think of myself as a mentor to most of my students, but I hope that they will be provoked by the conversations I instigate and by books that are difficult, or disorienting, or almost unbearably beautiful. *To the Lighthouse. The Marquise of O. The Unbearable Lightness of Being. Elizabeth Costello.* To mentor a student is to feel that you have been chosen to bring that student along in a way that is apt to be strenuous and potentially life changing, certainly for the student, and occasionally for the mentor. In a half century of teaching I have mentored no more than sixty or seventy students, and had Susan become a full-time teacher she would surely have found many students willing to be taken under her wing.

In the late 1980s, after the Albert Schweitzer Foundation announced it would establish a number of professorships at institutions of higher learning in New York State, the president of Skidmore College phoned and suggested we chat about this prospect. Competition for the limited number of Schweitzer professorships would be intense. The president asked if I could recommend a distinguished nominee who would have a real chance of winning an award for Skidmore. There's one, I suggested, explaining the nature of Susan's celebrity and the range of benefits she would bring to our students and faculty. Would she accept the nomination? Of that I wasn't certain, though I had reason to feel she would.

And thus was I authorized to "approach" her with the idea, bearing in mind that she was often in difficult financial straits, and had recently spoken to us of worries along those lines. The Schweitzer professorship would change all that. The annual salary, or stipend, was substantial, commensurate with the salary for an endowed university chair. The newly appointed professor was expected to remain in the position for at least five years, though she would be free to drop it if there were compelling reasons.

When I presented the idea to Susan at dinner one night in Manhattan, she was grateful and ebullient. A great idea! Was I sure that the college would want her? Of course, I was sure, and sure as well that the president was completely sold, feeling that Susan would be the ideal candidate for a college like ours, especially given her association with me and the fact that she appeared in public events at Skidmore at least once each year under my auspices. No doubt other schools would select strong nominees, but we were confident Susan would receive one of the coveted appointments. Though both of us had misgivings about mentorship, I believed she could do what was asked of her in spite of her skepticism about assuming that particular role and her ambivalence about the company of people who were in thrall to her.

In the following weeks, we spoke on the phone about the Schweitzer chair. I had reason to feel that Susan couldn't get it out of her mind, and was all but ready to say yes to the nomination. At one point, she asked me "to convey in writing some of the material concerning the Schweitzer chair," and on May 18, 1988, I sent her a detailed letter outlining the conditions and challenges. The money was, of course, a powerful factor. Though Susan received substantial speaking fees from many institutions, and her books sold well, she seemed to spend more than she could quite afford. I wondered about that, and Peg and I laughed at the fact that whenever Susan chose a restaurant for dinner it was apt to be an expensive one, with the Boyers expected to cover the bill, though in those days especially we were hardly affluent, with our oldest son in graduate school at Yale and two younger sons coming along.

In the end, Susan surprised us when she declared that she "just couldn't do it." Couldn't commit to what was entailed in the Schweitzer chair as I had described it. One undergraduate course each semester at Skidmore, with a limited enrollment. In addition, one faculty seminar each year, slated to meet six or eight times, with a theme and a modest reading list to be announced well in advance of the semester. Susan would have continued, of course, to live in Manhattan, but with a room at the college guest house, The Surrey Inn, free of charge, two or three nights each week during the academic year.

Susan was eloquent and persuasive in explaining why she

92

"just couldn't do it." For one thing—surely we knew this about her—she had a hard time pretending to sentiments she didn't have. The condition of her employment at Skidmore would require that she come to think of the students as "her kids" in a way that differed dramatically from the usual situation in which she faced them as an audience she'd not see again once she left campus. She'd often feel impatient or exasperated with students and begrudge the fact she was expected to suppress signs of her irritation. Worse, she would have to devise ways of trying to make them improve, to read more, to think more critically. "Not me," she would say. "Not that I couldn't do it, but it would take a toll."

Far worse was the idea of the faculty seminar, which she at first loved. In part her initial enthusiasm was rooted in her familiarity with some of my colleagues, whom she liked. Even when she spoke harshly to them in response to a question or a comment—"I know, I know," she said, "that I sometimes do that"—she thought she might come to see more in them if she spent time at Skidmore. One or two of them had even written about her work in ways that did not disappoint her.

All of these factors were part of "the problem," weren't they? We could see that, she was sure. Could see that once she was on campus, every week, with an office, and a schedule, there would be no escaping the faculty. Not just the students who would want a piece of her, but those professors who had signed up for her seminar, and wrote papers she would be expected to read and to discuss with them. "Those people," she said, "would more and more come to be in my head. I would have them in my head on the train back into Manhattan, and I might even find myself talking about them and their papers the way you talk about your own students, Robert, and really I can't have that happen. I don't want my head filled with 'those people,' not even if they're very good or very promising. Especially not if they're very good. Too many of them. Year after year they'd be there, and how could I just learn to ignore or forget them?"

Unanswerable, these reasons. So we felt when Susan laid them out. Sorry, she assured us, that after all we'll not be colleagues, and that we'll have to go on seeing one another the way we always have, once every other month or so. But we had to believe, she said, that she was right to decline the invitation.

That Susan was not disposed to be a teacher or a mentor was clearer than it had ever been. Clearer to me and to her. Truthfully, she had not been much of a teacher in her writing either. She wrote, for the most part, not to instruct but to declare an interest. To share a passion, to offer, as she said, "a theory of my own sensibility." When, early on, she derided critics who insisted upon sniffing around in books for meanings and truths and underlying intentions, she was essentially deriding the teacherly model adopted by generations of instructors who understood that above all they were required to teach students how to engage with a text. It was amazing, actually, that teachers who might well have felt she was describing them when she spoke of the "idea of content" and "interpretation" as a "not so subtle philistinism" nonetheless were charmed by her brashness and even her condescension. They were charmed too by insights that could seem almost absurdly peremptory, if not comically self-assured, as in her foreword to Robert Walser's *Selected Stories*, where she writes that "Kleist in Thun" is "an account of mental ruin as grand as anything I know," or describes Walser's virtues as "those of the most mature, most civilized art."[45] These are not teacherly observations, more like stimulants to ferment.

Still, in Susan's outlook a notable tension persisted, an ambivalence which she was never able to banish and rarely acknowledged, even an uncertainty as to what sort of critic she wished to be. Critics like George Steiner and Edmund Wilson often wrote frankly to instruct. When they introduced a new book in a review, they assumed their readers would come away better equipped to participate in a civilized conversation about influences, sources, salient characteristics. In their literary criticism, both Wilson and Steiner were fond of what Wilson called "narrative and drama as well as the discussion of comparative values." They often relied a good deal on the biographies of writers and artists and liked to tell stories that would illustrate the ideas they hoped to convey. Wilson wrote that he "tried to make it possible for our literate public to [better] appreciate and understand . . . [to] be able to deal with systems of art and thought that [may] have previously seemed inaccessible."[46] Even in writing for the *New Yorker*, as Wilson and Steiner did for many decades, both men were often teacherly in their intentions.

By contrast, until very late in her writing life, Susan did not often think of her role in this way. She wrote principally to discover, not so much to inform. Though she was not a poet, she thought of her criticism as having more in common with the prose of poets than with the critical essays of haute journalists like Wilson and Steiner. As she writes in a collection of essays, *Where the Stress Falls*, she admired the "fervor, velocity, fiber" in the prose of Joseph Brodsky, Marina Tsvetaeva, and Osip Mandelstam, identifying its component features of impatience, fondness for the elliptical, and willingness to employ "discontinuous or broken forms."

As was her habit, Susan made of her discovery a kind of theory, a somewhat theatrical generalization at once striking and more than a little dubious. "A poet's prose," she wrote, "is the autobiography of ardor" and the essays of poets express "a love for 'what is highest.'"[47] To think of such writing as predominantly instructional, explanatory, or analytic would be, in Susan's estimation, to misunderstand its very nature. She was not an Arnoldian critic handing out grades to works of art or underlining important moral imperatives, and she was not in any sense called to the vocation of the teacher who wrote to edify or educate the literate public.

Again, Susan was more ambivalent about her vocation than she let on. As early as "The Ideal Husband," her 1963 essay on Camus, she developed a telling distinction between the writer as lover and the writer as husband, concluding that Camus was "the ideal husband of contemporary letters," offering his readers such "solid virtues" as "reliability, intelligibility, generosity, decency."[48] By contrast, she argued, "the gifts of a lover" were temperamental. Women, she went on, pressing her point about as far as it might be driven, "tolerate qualities in a lover . . . that they would never countenance in a husband," and readers likewise tolerate in certain writers "unintelligibility, obsessiveness, painful truths, lies," so long as such writers "allow them to savor the rare emotions and dangerous sensations."

No reader of Sontag's essays will suppose that she was anything but compulsively drawn to varieties of extremity such as she invited us to associate with literary lovers and poets. No one will think of her as less than obsessive, excitable, insatiable. But just as surely she was drawn to order, intelligibility, and the other husbandly virtues. Even when her essays adopt the form of the elliptical or discontinuous, Susan is characteristically lucid and generous. She thought of herself as open to singularity, perversity, the limitless and incomprehensible, but in truth, as she conceded in the Camus essay, "as in life, so in art, both are necessary, husbands and lovers. It's a great pity when one is forced to choose between them."

Susan's reputation as a thinker open to the new and the experimental, together with her willingness to be thought excessive, rapturous, hortatory, infatuated, predisposed many readers to regard her late literary essays as tame, a falling off. In the posthumous volume, *At The Same Time: Essays and Speeches*, she includes several pieces written originally as introductions to new editions of a novel or nonfiction work. One such introduction is devoted to Leonid Tsypkin's novel *Summer in Baden-Baden*. The essay is marked throughout by a touching and uninhibited ardor. Susan is clearly writing, unashamedly, as an enthusiast, a devotee, willing to recommend and promote with all her vulnerable heart. Tsypkin's novel, she affirms, is "among the most beautiful, exalting, and original achievements of a century's worth of fiction." Its author wrote "for literature itself," and if you read his book, it may "fortify your soul and give you a larger idea of feeling, and of breathing."[49]

Obviously, Susan is thrilled with her discovery of an obscure book that might well have been lost to her and to "literature," a novel written in 1981 and issued twenty years later as a "lost masterpiece." Though she is alert to complexity in the book, her own attitude is resolutely uncomplicated, without any trace of an adversarial instinct. The lover here is in the first flush of her infatuation, entirely given over to her admiration, trusting her generosity, not at all moody or brutal, though with the poet-essayist's vital commitment to her own over-brimming ardor.

At the same time, much of the essay on Tsypkin patiently does the work of exposition, analysis, and instruction. Contexts are provided, the Russian scene outlined, Tsypkin's life history scrupulously sketched over several pages, the "true life" of Dostoyevsky matched against the ostensibly accurate account of the life given in the Tsypkin novel, in which Dostoyevsky is a central character. Susan's virtues in the essay are mainly the husbandly virtues. She makes the novel she recommends more intelligible than it would be without her assistance, and she happily endorses a work that is not itself committed to perversity, obscurity, or disorder. She notes the "emotional intensity" and "adamancy" of the work, but her essay has more to do with appreciation and instruction than with recommending dangerous emotions. Nowhere in the essay does she exploit her own personality in order to heighten her prose. Though she is drawn, inexorably, to sweeping assertions and to epithets like "amazing" and "uncanny," we cannot but feel that she offers us a reliably informed, decidedly useful pedagogic account.

Susan often was more of a teacher than she intended to be. And even where she wrote principally to discover what she thought, to test and exhibit the limits of her own sensibility—as any genuine critic ought to do—she betrayed the internal conflict she never quite resolved.

8 · MOTHERHOOD AND SEXUALITY

SUSAN never spoke to me of her sexuality. No doubt she assumed I knew what I knew, and was content not to pry. Perhaps I would have been as uncomfortable talking about her predilections as about my own. Neither did she open up to Peg about intimate matters on the rare occasions when the two of them would be out together for lunch when I was teaching an afternoon class or seeing a publisher in Manhattan. She had a discernible crush on Peg which was obvious to a number of our friends, and we were not surprised to hear from one of Susan's associates, just a year or two after her death, that she often spoke of her attraction to Peg. Will anyone believe me when I say I never cared much about Susan's sexuality? No more than I cared about the sexuality of other friends I saw frequently in New York, of Irving Howe or Richard Howard. Why should Susan's sexuality have mattered to me at a time when many of our gay friends had come out and were living fully satisfactory lives, holding academic positions and winning literary prizes? That Susan did not speak of herself as gay or bisexual did not matter to me, though I did wonder why she never introduced us to any of her lovers, and declined to write or be interviewed for the *Salmagundi* issue on homosexuality in 1981, declaring only that she would lose friends if she told what she knew.

One reason I rarely gave a thought to Susan's sexuality was that others talked about it openly, though only in passing, as if there were nothing secret or controversial about it. Still, her reluctance to allude to her own proclivities in no way interfered with her willingness to discuss gay liberation, or the politics of sexual identity, or the psychosexual charge in photographs by Robert Mapplethorpe. In fact, in her writings on Genet, Diane Arbus, and on Pauline Réage's *The Story of O*, Sontag had strikingly original things to say on the subject of sexuality. If Susan wished to maintain a private life to which some of us had no access, that was her decision. Was she more forthcoming about that private life when she was out to dinner with Richard Howard and David Alexander? Maybe so. But why would that have seemed unusual? Were there not certain friends with whom I shared more than I was apt to share with other friends?

But then several of our mutual friends noted, with some puzzlement, that Susan had refused, in interviews, to concede there was anything but "friendship" in her relations with her long-time lover and devoted companion Annie Leibovitz. This seemed inexplicable and disturbing to them. Benjamin Moser's account of Susan's thinking on this score makes her behavior even more incomprehensible. Certainly, it seemed incomprehensible to friends like Karla Eoff, who asked why Susan would care who knew about her sexual partners or lovers. Why, in particular, would a woman who had male lovers as well as female lovers be moved to deny her relations with Leibovitz? In Moser's account of the interview with Karla Eoff, Susan offered the following explanation:

Well, it's not like you, Karla. You can be married to a man, but it's not the same. We can't be devoted. Two

people of the same sex cannot be in the same relationship that people of the opposite sex are. And besides, I
still like men."

Pushed further, Susan says, "I don't think same-sex
relationships are valid. . . . The parts don't fit."[50]

Reading Susan's words, it is not hard to understand why she
didn't wish to talk about her private life. Why, even if things
said in rumors about her "were true," it seemed to her "uncivilized and vulgar" for anyone to repeat them. Uncivilized and
vulgar. Not the words anyone who admired the author of
"Notes on 'Camp'" in 1964 would have expected to hear from
her. But then who, forty years later, would have expected to
hear Susan say of her relations with women, "We can't be
devoted." Staggering! Though her explanations were not so
unusual for people of Susan's generation. Think of Michael
Specter's 2002 New Yorker profile of Larry Kramer, who "often
wondered in print why gay life had to be defined by sexual
promiscuity rather than by fidelity or love," and was "routinely
rejected" by the gay community.

Moser recounts that Susan was in terrible pain about many
aspects of her life and identity, about choices she had made and
failed to make. She was even conflicted about the benefit, or
the necessity, of holding on to a private life. She was, after all,
not merely a very public person but one who actively sought
and enjoyed publicity, who worked with publicists, had her
photograph taken with the beautiful and successful people,
and did little to ensure that her private life would remain private. Yet Susan was appalled by efforts to unearth secrets about
her life, though there were moments when she surely regarded
her fears of exposure as hysterical and excessive. Like many of
us she was not averse to taking in gossip, high and low. She was

deeply curious about our poet-friend Ben Belitt, a gay man whose view of homosexual relations—"We can't be devoted"— somewhat accorded with Susan's, though when we discussed his view with her she described it as an "anachronism." Her own anachronistic view of the matter was not a topic she ever cared to discuss with us.

It's difficult to determine what Susan really thought about privacy, apart from her wish to insist upon her own secrets when she was pressed. Did she believe in a sacred zone of privacy each of us is obliged to erect to protect what is most important about our lives and our loves? More than occasionally Susan would let down her guard and quietly open up to us about her fears. Fears of loneliness. Of being on her own in an emergency and finding that not very many people—of all those who sought her company—would be there for her when she most needed them.

Most often her fears had to do not with her own sexuality or loneliness but with her son David, unquestionably the one person she most admired and cared about. A relief, no doubt, for her to feel she could talk frankly with us about David, who was for a decade a regular columnist for *Salmagundi* and a teacher at the New York State Summer Writers Institute, where he had a devoted student following. Peg and I first met David in his twenties, but got to know him better when he began to write his early columns for *Salmagundi* and a series of first-rate books on Miami, LA, and the Bosnian war. Susan spoke often of my "good fortune" in having "persuaded David" to write for *Salmagundi* and teach at the Summer Writers Institute. "He is very brilliant, isn't he?" she would ask, knowing that I thought so and that our writer-friends thought so as well. She also spoke of his susceptibility to depression, and of her fear that she had been the cause of his troubles. "What do you do," she asked on more than one occasion, "when someone you love more than you love yourself does things you can't prevent? How can you undo what's already done?"

One aspect of her fear was generated by her awareness that although David was often the liveliest and wittiest person at a dinner or seminar table, he could also be condescending and disdainful of less compelling or accomplished people. "He isn't likable, is he?" Susan would sometimes say. "That's why they didn't give him the faculty appointment at Bard, isn't it? Why they gave it to a much less impressive person? He intimidates them, makes them feel somehow small. Don't you think?"

Impossible when confronted by these anxious musings not to agree that David, for all of his enormous attractiveness, could sometimes be a little terrifying. Though he could also be a sweet and playful companion, he had it in him to be cutting and dismissive. At the Summer Writers Institute dinners in our home, five nights each week in July, he would sit with other staff writers and be entirely companionable, until something would turn him, perhaps only the thought that the visiting writer scheduled to headline our evening event was not quite a writer he admired as much as fellow teachers like Marilynne Robinson, Francine Prose, Robert Pinsky, and Frank Bidart. As we neared the moment of departure for the campus event, David would conspire to persuade others at the table to stay put and let our special guest writer that evening discover what our staff writers thought of him or her. A paltry malevolence, and yet of a piece with other such displays to which David was susceptible.

Nor was this something rarely noted by others. Susan had heard about David's behavior often enough, and of course, when she was seated at the table with him, would find just that sort of casual condescension funny and irresistible. In fact,

David's superior airs were very much akin to qualities we often saw in Susan. Her fears that David would inevitably spoil his chances in life by proving to be unlovable and unpopular were surely related to fears she entertained about her own tendency to insult and drive away those who loved or admired her. Both of them could be patronizing, and it was only my enormous admiration for their work, and my love of Susan, that allowed me to put up with them. Not to mention the pleasure—the laughs—I would take from some of their arch pronouncements, as in David's opening remarks at a panel on American fiction: "I think that never in the history of intellectual life in America have the discussions of academics been more irrelevant to everything." "Can we go home now?" panelist Russell Banks asked by way of a first response.

Susan's gravest worries about David had to do with his cocaine habit. There was much Susan did not confide to me about what might have driven David to addiction, and the Moser biography is surely useful in providing the backstory, which includes tensions David was dealing with when he became his mother's editor at Farrar, Straus and Giroux. I saw nothing of the "decline" in David's work that others reported. His writing seemed as stylish and forceful as it had ever been, and though he had given up teaching at the Summer Writer's Institute, I saw him now and then in other settings, and he seemed always sharp, if also characteristically irritable. However, Susan was insistent that David was in trouble, and no doubt he was. She was also angry, and somewhat incredulous, that her son would risk everything—his health and his more than promising career as editor and writer—for something so tawdry.

Occasionally, Susan would regret her failure as a mother. Being a mother, she would say, seemed to her the most important thing she had done. At least she had wanted to believe that was true, but she knew she had not always believed it. Possibly, she said, if she had had more than one child, the pressures David felt as her son would not have been so overwhelming. She spoke most often of the period of David's bout with addiction, when she alternated between recrimination and rue. Once, when she spent an afternoon alone with Peg at the Metropolitan Museum of Art, and the conversation turned to David, she told her that it was wrong to have only one child, and that Peg really had to have at least one more. Right away.

Absolutely no one who knew Susan would have described her as motherly. But then, she wasn't much like anyone else, ever, and never fit into any conventional role. "She really wanted to be a great mother," Jamaica Kincaid said, "but it was sort of like wanting to be a great actress, or something. The mechanics of being a mother were really beyond her. It's like if you put her on Mars and they spoke another language. She had no real instinct for it. I would say there was no real instinct for caring about another person unless they were in a book."[51]

9 · RHAPSODE

I

T was no secret that Susan aspired to be a filmmaker and made several films which many of her friends thought disappointing. While she wrote some of the best essays ever devoted to films and film directors, the directors she chose as models in no way served her own filmmaking needs. Unfortunately, she read into the works of directors she admired a thesis that almost amounted to a programmatic rejection of features essential to the success even of avant-garde films she so admired. We spoke of this programmatic imperative on several occasions. Susan never conceded that this was more than a figment of my own more sober, limited, rationalist perspective. There was never anything remotely programmatic, she asserted, in her approach to works of art.

Around the time she published her seminal 1967 essay on Ingmar Bergman's *Persona*, I published my own ambitious take on the film. Though my contacts with her at this point were mainly epistolary, we did have two phone conversations, in one of which she noted that my essay seemed to have been written "expressly to contradict" hers. She wasn't finger-wagging or defensive. She was riding high at that moment as the most admired critic in the country, while, at twenty-six, I was still finding my way and publishing the Bergman essay in my fledgling *Salmagundi*. It was generous of Susan to respond to that issue, which I had sent her, and to notice that we did regard the

Bergman film in drastically different ways. For decades, I have taught *Persona* again and again, and always assigned Susan's essay, encouraging my students to discover for themselves—though with my framing and questions—what may be said to support or refute her primary thesis. Never have I alerted them to my own essay, which is no match for Susan's as a work of literary prose, and seemed to me, almost from the first, academic and clunky, though I continue to believe in my reading of the film.

Susan had an inveterate tendency to praise artists and artworks she admired, a wonderful, generous instinct obvious in her essays and in her personal demeanor. While browsing with us at a record store in Manhattan, she found an LP of the Chausson Piano Trio and, bubbling over with encouragement, insisted that we buy it at once. In her 2001 Preface to *Letters Summer 1926*, she celebrates the writing of three poets—Boris Pasternak, Rainer Maria Rilke, and Marina Tsvetaeva—who later became "future gods," and added that we must not "dismiss as 'romantic'" their "purity of aspiration." After all, she gushed, the letters of these poets give us "angelic conversation," all the more essential at a time when opera alone remains a medium where "it is still acceptable to rhapsodize."

Susan's instinct to rhapsodize was an aspect of a certain extravagance that could invite several species of exaggeration. Her inspired, over the top take on Hans Jürgen Syberberg's film *Our Hitler* drove some of her readers to refer to the film as "Her Hitler." Exaggeration was also an aspect of her commitment to modernist aesthetics and the avant-garde posture, to the difficult and opaque. She wished to be, and to remain, ahead of her reader, willing to be understood but not to confirm a prejudice or to be thought merely pleasing. Her early assault on "interpretation" was bracing and beneficial and yet lent itself to a kind of denial when it came to artwork that clearly invited interpretation. Her essay on *Persona* uses the film to make a case for qualities like "opacity" and "multiplicity," and warns against going "behind" a work of art to find a meaning that "resides in the work itself." The case for those virtues, including opacity and indecipherability, has never been made more beautifully than in Susan's essay, and each time I read it with my students, we are entirely at one in finding it thrilling.

But *Persona* is not indeterminate in the way Susan suggests, and the audience for the film is not, as she would have it, haunted by "the sense of a lost or absent meaning" to which there is no access. There is no need for a viewer to go "behind" the film to differentiate between dream and reality or to identify the links between apparently unconnected episodes. Susan's insistence on withheld information leads her to overstate the difficulty of deciphering aspects of a film which is indeed an avant-garde performance and yet not defiantly opaque.

Years after our respective essays appeared, when we were friends and saw one another fairly often, she asked me whether I seriously believed that everything in *Persona* could be accounted for in the way I had suggested, and I invited her to come with me one day to a classroom where I would go through the film frame by frame with students—students who would be armed with her essay. She thought that would be fun, though we never tried hard enough to make that visit happen.

We might well have arranged another classroom visit for a session built on Godard's *The Married Woman*, about which I wrote another essay, again arguing that Susan's take on the avant-garde nature of Godard's work was unduly programmatic.[52] Though we never sat together for a film-class dissection of the Godard film, Susan did "like" my essay, though she asked me, a smile on her face, if I thought that everything in the film "added up." Did I not see that such confidence on my part went against the grain of Godard's aesthetic and made his film much more deliberate and predictable than it was? In our conversations I was less certain about my view of the avant-garde, and after reading Susan's inspired essays on Godard, I always felt she understood—far better than I could—the experimental recklessness that made his work so vital to our generation.

Susan's readiness to embrace indeterminacy and obliquity sometimes led her to other assertions that seemed dubious to me. At a panel discussion on "Difficulty" one July afternoon at the Summer Writers Institute, I asked her about an assertion she often made, namely, that so-called "traditional narrative" routinely aspires to provide "full satisfaction of one's desire to know." By contrast, she asserted, we appreciate impenetrable works not conceived with "the old expectations." It was not surprising, I said, that Susan would make such a case, at a time when she was working to open a way to further appreciation of artworks that were opaque or indeterminate in their pur-poses. But surely she didn't think that novels like *Anna Karenina, Fathers and Sons,* or *Madame Bovary* aspire to make us believe that all the essential questions have been answered, all motives accounted for, all mysteries dispelled. Wasn't this a misleading way of underlining the differences between "traditional" works and the modernist novels she championed?

Susan was generous in response, though a bit puzzled by my insistence that traditional narrative was anything but deter-mined to answer the questions it sets in motion.

"Of course," she declared, "those novels don't answer in so many words every single question. But don't they send a reader home feeling content that the main issues have been resolved? Wasn't that the key to their success?"

"Maybe so," I countered, "and yet that depends on what you mean when you say 'resolved.'" At which point we agreed to disagree—just a little—about several figures in the novels I had named. Susan clearly enjoyed a comradely dispute without feeling disparaged.

However, Susan was not always amenable to debate. Often she bristled at nothing. At anything. And she was especially inclined to bristle when she suspected she was being consigned to the status of critic or even woman of letters. Though I made it clear to her that I admired her late novels, both *The Volcano Lover* and *In America*, from which she read at public events I sponsored, she never felt that I or her other friends understood the nature of her achievement in those works. Why, she asked, did I not find a way to write about *In America* for one of the national magazines, when I had sung its praises to her?

"Come on, admit it," she once said. "You do continue to think of me as a critic. You do."

"Well," I said, on more than one occasion, "I don't think of you as a critic exactly, but as one of the very greatest of American essayists. And I don't know why that wouldn't please you."

"If you don't know," Susan said, "then there's no hope, and I won't even try to explain it to you."

It was one thing for Susan to tell me, at our kitchen table, in a restaurant, on a comradely walk, that there was no hope I'd understand something I should have understood. I was accustomed to absorbing her disapproval, more often than not taking it to heart, thinking she was probably right. However, there was no way I could make myself believe that Susan Sontag would be remembered principally as filmmaker, novelist, or playwright. I did think the late novels a tremendous advance over her earlier fiction, and believed a few of her short stories were first rate, especially "The Way We Live Now." But Susan would want to be compared not to the young novelist who had written *The Benefactor*, her first novel, but to writers who had composed supremely beautiful and moving works—like José Saramago's *The Year of the Death of Ricardo Reis* or W. G. Sebald's *Austerlitz*. Far better, I thought, far more appropriate, to think of her as an author whose book *On Photography* was the best of its kind, as someone who had taught a generation how to think more honestly about subjects like illness, torture, and pornography than had ever seemed possible. She was, at her best—and she was often at her best—as an essayist who could take her place at the table with her chosen masters, with Walter Benjamin and Elias Canetti, Roland Barthes and Simone Weil, Lionel Trilling and Elizabeth Hardwick.

When I introduced her once or twice each year at a public event, I would speak of her principally as essayist. Even when she had told me that she'd be reading from a novel, or from her play *Alice In Bed*, I'd mention the new work, prepare the audience to receive it, but extol Susan as a major essayist, as a thinker and intellectual who had shaped the way we thought about our culture. On one occasion, she waited for the applause to die down after my introduction, stepped to the microphone, and looking out over faces that included many of my writer friends, proceeded to tear me to pieces. "Robert Boyers still doesn't get it," she declared. "After how many years doing this, he still doesn't get it. Doesn't get that I'm a novelist and that all this other writing he talked about is writing I did to keep writing and have something to do while I was developing myself as a fiction writer."

Of course, I had seen Susan tear into others before. Had occasionally risen to someone else's defense when I felt that

Susan had gone too far or couldn't restrain herself. But there was something about this occasion that felt different, perhaps because I was Susan's host, and knew that my friends in the front rows would be seething with anger on my account. Would I say something after the public part of the evening ended? Would I allow Susan to take my arm as we walked to the reception or pretend that nothing unusual had occurred?

The moment Susan stepped away from the podium Peg approached her and said, "You must apologize to Robert immediately—and don't pretend that you don't know what you did that requires an apology. Just apologize, and mean it."

We got through the evening, as always, and of course Susan didn't know that what she had done was hurtful or that it amounted to anything to worry over. She knew that I was a person who, when he loves and admires someone, can forgive, and forgive again. She knew that I would be grateful for our years of friendship and struggle, and would think that her work entitled her to behave as only a great writer was entitled to. No doubt she also knew that I would not defend such a view of the great writer, and would spend occasional sleepless nights tallying her virtues and hopelessly measuring them against her unbecoming qualities. Would think, even now, of the inscription she wrote—"In Fealty, from Susan"—in a volume of Annie Leibovitz photographs she gave to us one evening a year before her death, and wonder what such an inscription might have meant to her. But then I'm far more inclined to second the impulse of Janet Malcolm, to let misgiving and unpleasantness "recede in significance when viewed against the vast canvas" of all that Susan gave us.[53]

TWO

Impossible to Tell: George Steiner

" . . . *the eternal problem of attachment.*"
PHILIP ROTH

"*Relationships should make us feel better. Why else bother? But there are different ways of feeling better.*"
ADAM PHILLIPS

1 · A FIRST MEETING

I FIRST met George Steiner in early September 1965 at the bar in the One Fifth Avenue Hotel in Manhattan. I was almost twenty-three. He and his illustrious colleague, the Irish diplomat and author Conor Cruise O'Brien, were to interview me for a seat in a New York University Graduate Seminar on the literature of the European political right. The two Albert Schweitzer Professors had read my application, as well as two short writing samples I'd appended, both from the pages of *Dissent* magazine, one on Peter Weiss's play *Marat/Sade*, the other a review of O'Brien's recent collection of essays on politics and literature.

"Slight," was Steiner's word for these pieces, "very slight."

"He's just starting out, George," said O'Brien, shifting in his bar stool to make room for me to squeeze in between them. "You mustn't worry too much about things that my friend George says," O'Brien went on. "He admired what you wrote, especially about the *Marat/Sade*, though he won't want you to know that."

George seemed to me then, and later, a hard man. Hard in the sense that he often asked you to be equal to demands you couldn't meet. Expected you to have read books you couldn't possibly have read, proved yourself original to a degree that was clearly beyond you. Nothing about George was circumspect or cautious. He spoke with a brusque, sometimes abrasive, confidence. He seemed to have read (and remembered) everything and to have thought every thought. With little warning he came out with lengthy quotations: passages from Hegel, or Kierkegaard, entire poems by Goethe or Baudelaire or Browning. He was always one or two steps ahead of anyone, springing nimbly from one idea to another, enlarging a point you had made, correcting a slip. Often at the front of his utterances were the words "of course." OF COURSE, you were familiar with recent developments in psycholinguistics. OF COURSE, you understood that Keats's equation of truth and beauty could not be demonstrated in the sphere of music. OF COURSE, you'd considered that, when it is mutually attained, orgasm is a kind of simultaneous translation.

In our initial interview George expressed astonishment that I had applied for a seat in the seminar without having a mastery of German. "But we'll be reading everything in English translation, George," said O'Brien, "and it's clear the boy has read his Nietzsche and even his *Doctor Faustus*. My god, George, but I can tell that he's even been reading you."

More than a little nervous about spending two semesters in the company of the formidable Steiner—he was, at that early stage of his career, the author of two major books and numerous controversial essays eventually collected in *Language and Silence*—I was admitted to the seminar, and felt I would be equal to its demands. Stirred by the readings and by sharp exchanges between Steiner and O'Brien, I soon realized this course would be the most challenging academic experience of my life. But Steiner was determined that no one at our table should feel comfortable. Was I aware that Isaiah Berlin's essay on Joseph de Maistre, which I had cited, was by no means the last word on that subject? I did understand, did I not, that many philosophers, from Plato to Sartre, had been attracted to despotism, that it was not only Nietzsche or Heidegger who were drawn to hierarchy and tyranny. Yes, yes, Thomas Carlyle, why not bring him in, by all means, you seem to have read him carefully, though he's not at the level of the others we're studying. You know that, yes?

But, these challenges were the least of the difficulties I encountered. More troubling by far were the moments when Steiner would suddenly ask me to respond to a passage he quoted, from Novalis, or Schopenhauer, in their original German.

"But Professor Steiner," I would say, pathetic and embarrassed, "you do recall surely that at our interview I made it very clear I had a less than elementary command of German."

"That he did, George," said O'Brien, "and I dare say that not more than one or two others at this table would be able to do what you're asking of Boyers."

"Hard to believe," George insisted, "that Boyers and those others would take up seats at the table when there were so many—no doubt with better German—who applied and were turned away."

"I'm afraid you'll just have to live with it, George," said O'Brien, "and we will all have to live with you, won't we?"

When I met Steiner, I was about to launch the first issue of *Salmagundi*, which has been central to my work and my friendships since 1965. Three years after the seminar I asked him to contribute to a special issue on the legacy of the German refugee intellectuals, and soon after that we became improbable friends. He went on to write frequently for *Salmagundi*—almost two dozen essays over the years. For more than five decades my wife, Peg, and I saw him at least once each year, in New York, in London, in Rome, and elsewhere. Twice each month for more than fifty years we exchanged letters. When George delivered the six Charles Eliot Norton Lectures at Harvard in the fall of 2001, we drove to Boston each week to join the many hundreds of people in attendance. Often he came to Skidmore College at my invitation, participating in conferences and delivering memorable lectures on subjects ranging from *Antigone* to "The Dreyfus Case" and "The Responsibility of Intellectuals." Some lectures were delivered without notes.

I repeat that our friendship was, in several respects, improbable. George was an *haute* European intellectual who rightly regarded me as hopelessly American, despite my efforts to absorb and even write about the work of demanding European thinkers. He never came to terms with my love of baseball and football, the pleasure I took in playing tennis on selected weeknights with my wife and friends at an indoor facility. Though we shared a passion for the novels of Nadine Gordimer and the paintings of Johannes Vermeer, there were reaches of George's mandarin erudition that remained decidedly foreign to me. At times, George was encouraging about the books and articles I wrote, but he could also be withering. When I wrote in the *New Republic* an ungenerous review of Thomas Bernhard's novel *The Loser*, George fired off a scolding letter asking how I could have thought myself a suitable reviewer for such a book. When a favorable review of my book on Lionel Trilling appeared on the front page of the *Times Literary Supplement* in 1977, George wrote to ask why neither I nor the reviewer, John Bayley, had noted my failure to address the "obviously central" question of Trilling's ambivalent relation to Judaism.[54]

Why did I put up with George? For beginners, I admired his drive, his erudition, his work ethic, and I was grateful he saw something admirable in me. Much that he wrote and said opened doors that would have remained closed for me, and his example made me want to be a better writer, to read more and risk more. As our friendship deepened I came to regard as incidental what was harsh or ungenerous in him. Though he had it in him to be brutal, and I knew that brutality is never innocent, he was never gratuitously brutal towards me, and I found it rather easy to love what was lovable in him. My psychoanalyst friend Leslie H. Farber said that the key to my relations with George and with Susan Sontag—"and no doubt with others"—was my "gift for admiration." Remembering that, I think now of something Farber wrote in a passage on Kierkegaard, that "envy was unhappy self-assertion, while admiration was happy self-surrender." A danger, to be sure, some varieties of self-surrender, but then we don't always get to choose among the implacably compelling sentiments that take hold of us— like the love I felt for George even in the face of challenges that might well have turned off someone else. "The unpredictable nature of love," Farber wrote, "which, unlike other desirable things that we are told life has in store for the deserving, refuses to be earned, discriminates arbitrarily and according to a private standard."[55]

2 · "I HAD A GOOD TIME"

GEORGE and Susan rarely saw one another. Neither was enthusiastic about the other, both surprised to be members of our extended "family." When I first thought of bringing them together I suspected such a meeting would not go well. But then Susan had begun asking all sorts of questions about George. She heard that he was exhausting to be with, that he told people he had read everything worth reading. What did I make of his references to higher mathematics and to thinkers only he had ever heard of? Did he ever try to respond to the attacks leveled at him at the *Salmagundi* conference built around his "The Archives of Eden" essay, when several speakers—Susan among them—disputed almost everything he wrote about American culture?[56]

For his part, George grew more and more curious about Susan, and wondered at the extraordinarily diverse following she had managed to sustain. In a number of her comments at the "Archives of Eden" conference she had seemed, he believed, to second his key insights, though it was clear that, like other speakers, she thought his dim, largely dismissive, view of American culture misleading. In May 1981, I wrote Susan that I had spent a day with George two weeks earlier, and told her that he "wants very much to get to know you," in fact asks me "to bring the two of you together when he's in New York next fall." I went further, assuring her that "he speaks of you with an unambivalent admiration that is new for him." Yes, he had a reputation for being overbearing, but I was all but certain that both would "have a fine time" together. Did I believe that? In truth, George was improbably gregarious and even jolly when he was enjoying himself, and I found it impossible to suppose that he would not, in every sense, rise to the occasion when seated at a table with Susan under friendly auspices. He liked what she had lately written about a number of writers—Elias Canetti and Walter Benjamin especially—he, too, had championed. Peg and I were optimistic our efforts to gather them under our wing would prove successful.

Despite her bemused skepticism about George's feats of learning and his extravagant self-presentation, Susan agreed that it was time they met, "at leisure, at length," and she would find it bearable only if Peg and I "presided." Though I proposed one or two other guests we might invite to join us, Susan insisted that we plan the dinner for the four of us. "I want to experience your friend George for myself," she said in the course of a long telephone conversation, "to see whether he's as intolerable as I'm told he is. To find out whether he can ever stop talking."

We all met at a restaurant in lower Manhattan, where the conversation, over nearly six hours, was strenuous but amiable. Nothing nasty. No sly innuendo. Here and there questions about Susan's son, David, and George's children. About George's decision to teach at the University of Geneva and his relations with the *New Yorker*'s "Mister Shawn." Only once a potentially treacherous turn, in the direction of Susan's former husband, Philip Rieff, and our sponsorship of his work on "Psychological Man" in the pages of *Salmagundi*. Though Susan wondered—not for the first time—about our commitment to that body of work, George made it clear that he regarded Philip

Rieff as "something close to a major thinker," and reminded Susan that he was by no means alone in this, noting that there were writers Susan admired—Christopher Lasch, Alasdair MacIntyre, and Norman O. Brown among them—who shared George's view of Rieff.

"Casaubon," Susan said. "When I think of him I think of George Eliot's Casaubon."

"But this Casaubon is anything but a dry stick," George said.

"Oh come on," Susan fired back. "He postures, George. His gravity about the modern condition is an affectation, his intelligence is antiquarian," Susan insisted.

"I can see that you've not recovered from him, not yet," George replied.

We parted at one in the morning, George walking back to a nearby hotel, Susan strolling with us to our car so we could drive her to her apartment. Her assessment was that the evening had been a success, that she and Steiner had managed to say "real things" to one another and that George had been "on his best behavior." Though it was exhausting, wasn't it, to confront for so many hours that "barrage of unchecked eloquence"? Her head hurt, Susan confessed. It was a pleasurable experience, but still, painful. We spoke, briefly, of George's will to performance, and agreed that his will to perform had been brought to a pitch of intensity by his desire to impress someone who arrived thinking him pompous and tedious. "But we'll do it again," Susan declared. "You'll bring us together again and make it tolerable. And you'll tell him that I had a good time."

When we joined George for dinner the next night he had much the same impression of the evening with Susan, and when I wrote to Susan a day later I assured her that "George couldn't stop talking about how well it all went. . . . He's always on, needless to say . . . but I hope you agree that a lot of it is first-rate conversation."

I knew it took a lot for Susan to get over her feelings about George, that she was pre-disposed not to like him, and much that she said about him would continue to have a competitive edge. It was no secret that, for all of their differences of style and outlook, they were frequently drawn to the same issues and shared a sense of which writers and thinkers most demanded attention. "A new book by George Steiner is always an event," wrote a reviewer for the *New York Times*, and that was true as well for any new book or essay by Susan. George could never match Susan's celebrity. She knew that, and yet the competitive instincts persisted. Impossible to forget a phone call she made to Peg one night in 1994, when her long-awaited *Paris Review* interview had just appeared. "Can you believe," she fumed, "that the editors put their interview with me in the same issue as their Steiner interview? Was this their idea of a joke?"

To which Peg could only say, "Maybe they thought you had more in common than either of you is willing to admit."

"That's not very funny," Susan said, though soon she and Peg shared a laugh about temper tantrums and bad behavior. Hers and George's.

We brought George and Susan together on several subsequent occasions, twice at *Salmagundi* conferences when their sons, David Rieff and David Steiner, were with them. On other occasions, they were less friendly and forgiving. In the Netherlands, I was invited to preside at a session of a 2001 "Nexus Institute" featuring George and Susan, my assignment "to prevent the two of them from tearing one another to pieces," as our host, Rob Rieman, put it to me in a phone conversation. He had heard that relations between George and Susan had cooled, worsened, though exactly why, he could not say, and of course I knew that "cooled" was putting it mildly. I had spoken before at Nexus conferences, and was not surprised when Rieman told me it had long been his ambition to feature George and Susan on the same platform. Nor was I surprised to learn that each of them had spoken harshly of the other when Rieman phoned them and that both had agreed to participate on the condition that I chair their public session. Not a good idea, I told Rieman. Not necessary to have them on stage together, when they had decided that their relationship, such as it was, had shattered and was beyond repair. George assured me, when we spoke about the Nexus conference during some days together on vacation in Milan, that he would be "perfectly civil," though he detailed what he took to be Susan's inexcusable lapses and her cavalier indifference to the favors he had lavished upon her. When Peg contacted Susan, she said that none of this was a big deal and that she had other things more important to think about.

On a warm May evening before the conference opened, we checked into a pleasant hotel in Tilburg and gathered with other participants in a large dining hall. For a while Peg and I stood and chatted with Susan and the Polish writer Adam Zagajewski, impatient for George to arrive and get past the initial greetings and the inevitable tensions. But George came in just as dinner was served, and we moved to take our assigned seats next to him at a long table. Would he like to amble over to Susan's table, across the room, and break the ice? No, he would not, George said, though I should not be anxious. All would be well at the panel. "Madame" would behave herself, and so would he.

Shortly before nine the next morning Peg boarded the bus chartered to take us to the conference center and saw George seated up front, right behind the driver. He called to her to sit beside him, and when I boarded, perhaps ten minutes later, I took a seat four or five rows back. Within a minute or so Susan climbed up, looked at George, extended her hand and called out, loudly, "Hello, George, it's Susan. It's good to see you," a gesture George entirely ignored. Again Susan called to him, and again George continued to stare out the window, coiled away from Susan's outstretched hand, so that Peg scolded George in Italian and told him that he was required to be civil and try at least to do what he had promised, though to no avail. At which point Susan raised her voice still further, demanding that George at least acknowledge her, until, despairing, she cast her eyes over the small sea of others looking on with amazement. "Robert," she suddenly called to me, in an imperious and yet pleading voice, "you see that your friend Steiner up here refuses to take my hand and won't even say hello to me. I want you to come up here and make him acknowledge me. Please, come up here and make him do that." At which point I stood up and, with others in the bus, told Susan to just stop and take a seat back with us—which reluctantly, after a moment of further hesitation, she did, while George remained unreachable, stony and implacable.

What to make of such a spectacle? Seated next to me a few minutes later, Susan confessed that she didn't know what had come over her. Did I know what had so incensed George as to cause him to behave so badly? Yes, I knew, and told her. She had asked him to send her two rare and expensive books through the good offices of a bookseller in Geneva. That he had done. She had asked for additional favors, and never thanked him, nor answered the two substantial letters he had sent her, nor paid the bookseller for those costly volumes. This he thought unforgivable. And why, she asked, would he not simply complain or berate her instead of indulging this childish behavior? Because he did complain, I told her, in those letters he sent her, and he had been ignored. And you, she asked. Would you have behaved in this way if I had neglected you? You always answer my letters, I said, or phone me. And anyway, we have a different sort of history. George has always felt that you dislike and mistrust him. And here he finds that you have confirmed his opinion. That you don't think enough of him to thank him for his favors or acknowledge his existence.

I feared there was more and worse to come that day. At the late afternoon session in Tilburg, an audience of a thousand people, with no sense of the tensions animating the principal speakers, would surely have been astonished to witness a display of venomous antipathy. But at the public session, both Susan and George spoke eloquently of the relation between art and politics, of commemoration and the difficulty entailed in bearing witness to extremity. So too did the other principal speaker, Peter Eisenman, architect of the controversial Berlin Holocaust memorial, whose steadying presence on the panel I welcomed. For a while all seemed to be going well enough, until Susan spoke of her own time in Sarajevo during the Bosnian war, and suggested that her experience there amounted to something obviously different in kind from anything other artists and writers might draw upon to anchor their thoughts on extremity. Was this not so? Of course, it was so, said George, staring at Susan, and, of course, Susan had exhibited at Sarajevo and at other places, in other times, a courage and ferocity of determination that a person like himself could only wonder at. Always he had felt that there was a dimension of personal, even physical, courage and generosity in Susan's commitment to bearing witness that was exemplary and simply out of reach for most of us, himself very much included.

Though George had never spoken to me of Susan's exemplary virtues before, this turn in the conversation seemed entirely genuine, and was received as such by Susan. By no means a prelude to some impending rapprochement, George's words were on everyone's minds at the reception following the event, where he and Susan stayed well away from one another and never thought it necessary or appropriate to shake hands and definitively put an end to their ongoing hostilities. On the bus back to our hotel, Peg told George that she had never fully appreciated what a terrific chess player he was, that he now seemed to her someone especially adept at anticipating an opponent's moves and playing to win without placing his foot on his opponent's neck.

"You've never once seen me play chess, my dear," said George.

"Well," said Peg, "I've read your Fischer-Spassky book, and throughout I imagined you playing through the moves."

"An amateur," said George. "I'm a rank amateur, nothing more."

"Well," said Peg, "it may be that the move you just made up there with Susan was your greatest performance as a chess master—amateur or not."

"Do you think she admired it as much as you did?" George asked.

"You know, George, you could ask her yourself," Peg said.

3 · UNDER ATTACK

GEORGE was always in the eye of one storm or another. He attracted criticism of a peculiarly vitriolic kind. Even among friends of mine who admired his work and were in awe of his learning and panache, there was a tendency to laugh at his flamboyance, his willingness to come out with a pronouncement certain to astonish, his sheer *chutzpah*. Where Susan often drew criticism for making incendiary and provocative statements ("The white race is the cancer of human history"),[57] George's detractors frequently accused him of taking on subjects he could not possibly have mastered ("The notion that one can exercise a rational literacy ... without a knowledge of calculus, without some preliminary access to topology or algebraic analysis, will soon seem a bizarre archaism").[58] But then George really did impress scholars of Russian literature with his *Tolstoy or Dostoevsky*, in spite of his having no Russian. He did seem to classical scholars to write a first-rate book about *Antigone* without the training of a classicist. He also composed a compelling book on Heidegger for the Fontana Modern Masters series without having the credentials of an academic philosopher. At international symposia, his sustained reflections on the Hebrew Bible, on the relation between the last supper of Socrates and the last supper of Jesus were central to the debates conducted by biblical scholars. Occasionally, I would write letters to editors to correct some preposterous imputation, and traded blows with one opponent or another on George's behalf in the pages of the *New York Times Book Review* or the *New Criterion*. I never knew how much the attacks directed at him, some of them mocking, stayed with George, and never knew him to be inclined to answer attacks, not even when they were obviously inspired by *ressentiment* or sheer malice. George understood that he was a public intellectual, and that many would necessarily envy his position as regular book reviewer for the *New Yorker* and as a scholar-critic whose books would routinely reach academic *and* general audiences. One afternoon, at a Harvard university seminar attended by six or seven academics—he had been invited to lecture that evening, but accepted the invitation to an additional "intimate" meeting with a handful of faculty—George was asked whether he was as conversant with the major Christian theologians as his casual allusions would suggest. "Try me," George said, and proceeded then to speak comfortably and eloquently of Pascal and Kierkegaard, of Augustine and Aquinas.

In several respects the oddest of all the attacks directed at George was leveled at him by Edward Said in the *Nation* magazine in 1985. At that time Said was himself one of the most prominent intellectuals in the world, and though I don't know if his lectures and public appearances typically drew the crowds that George routinely attracted, Said certainly had a large following on the political and academic left, and his books were taught in many undergraduate and graduate courses, including mine. George thought Said's *Orientalism* was easy to misread and misuse, that its targets were chosen with a cavalier disregard for important distinctions, as if all Western scholars presuming to deal with the Arab world were apt to be guilty of the same missteps and omissions. An irony, George said on more than one occasion, that a first-rate mind like Said, incensed at "monolithic" Western views of Islam, would adopt a monolithic view of Western scholars presuming to take on Arab history and culture. George conceded that I had been fortunate to publish Said's best early work in *Salmagundi*, and he mischievously reminded me that Said's first wife, Maire Kurrik—herself a professor and distinguished scholar—had told me in a phone conversation that she understood very little of what her husband had written for us—"and neither do you," she had said.

Said's essay for the *Nation* magazine was a lengthy review of *George Steiner: A Reader*, a volume which collected some of George's best writings, among them the early essays from *Language and Silence*, and substantial excerpts drawn from *Tolstoy or Dostoevsky, The Death of Tragedy, After Babel, Martin Heidegger*, and other works. Said's review began with this salvo: "In George Steiner's case, the first things to be said about him are at once the most obvious and, I think, the least important. You cannot avoid his colossal pomposity and egotism. . . . Neither," Said wrote, "can it be doubted that there are 'anti-Steinerians.'"[59] Why so? Steiner's "public pose" was widely considered to be "overdeveloped and obtrusive," his generalizations often "absurdly theatrical." He "paraded" his work "before us in the manner of Aristotle contemplating the bust of Homer in a café on the Danube, to the strains of Schönberg, Greek dirges and screams." In short, Said set off determined to produce his own bona fides as one entirely in step with the "anti-Steinerians," persons, presumably, with wit, an aversion to pomposity, and a deep suspicion of intellectuals whose theatricality and range seemed to them a mark of unseemly, even absurd, ambition. Though Said didn't say so, his devastating opening paragraph echoed, in important respects, the leaden, thoroughly uninspired resentment of George that circulated in academic literary circles in Britain, where his championing of comparative literature studies, his gall in presuming to take on subjects outside the standard framework of "English studies," and his enormous stature among "general readers" were felt to be an affront to good sense and a decent, middling modesty of outlook. I heard variations on this theme back in the sixties when I first met George, and I heard it again in the seventies when I began writing frequently for the *Times Literary Supplement* and met a number of good, gray British academics who would ask me, with a note of bemusement, "What is your friend Steiner up to these days?"

But Said was no ordinary academic, and his review quickly made a turn that would surely have bewildered those in the British literary establishment for whom George was always an affront to their own mild ambitions. After all, Said wrote, Steiner's "faults are not the disabilities of mediocrity." He had been "a brilliant reproach" to his critics, and was, without question, "that rare thing, a critic propelled by diverse enthusiasms, a man able to understand the implications of trends in different fields, an autodidact for whom no subject is too arcane." Was he a strange bird? He was, but then "Steiner is to be read for his quirks, rather than in spite of them." He wrote works applauded by major scholars in the several different disciplines to which he had devoted books and essays, and yet it was no small accomplishment that he wrote also "to be understood by non-specialists." It was not a weakness but a major strength that "his terms of reference" were "trilingual, eccentric and highly urbane," and that he took his lead from nothing "as stable as doctrine or authority." If he was an egotist there was an "other side of his egotism: that he, George Steiner, conscientiously tries to register every response accurately, work through every difficulty, test every feeling, authenticate each experience of the best that is known and thought."

In fact, Said argued, though George was not always at his best, he was "without peer" in several of the domains he entered. To his credit, in his writings on Jewish history and culture and his reflections on Israel, Steiner exhibited a "stubborn Diaspora ethic" which was "a salutary counter to the pieties and callousness of dogmatic American Zionism." Moreover, Steiner was enormously informative and original in his "discussions of language and translation," most impressively in *After Babel*, where "the learning and insight . . . are remarkably exhilarating." Steiner's insights "into writers unhoused in or dislodged from any single language are superb ones," Said had written in another review published in the *New York Times Book Review*.[60] If George was theatrical and "obtrusive," it was also obvious that no one else on the Anglo-American scene had done so well what for many years he had been doing. "The rare thing," Said wrote, was "that he puts himself at the inner core of a discourse, discipline, language, author, and then communicates outward to the uninitiated, without losing either the intimacy or the urgent clarity of each realm." There is always, Said concludes, "much to be learned from what he says," and "much pleasure" in reading him.

The day Said's review appeared in the *Nation*, Said phoned to alert me. Though we had spoken on several occasions, he was not a friend of mine, and had only called me once before. I was surprised that he thought it necessary to ask if I'd seen the current issue of the *Nation*, but I understood completely when he said that his piece contained a few sentences that "your friend Steiner won't like."

"He's a big boy," I replied.

"Oh but I mean," Said insisted, "these are sentences he is

bound to dislike in a way that could spell trouble for all of us next weekend." When I asked him to read the sentences, he said he would prefer that I read them for myself, in context. The words "next weekend" referred to the fact that we were to convene for three days at Skidmore College for a *Salmagundi* magazine conference on "intellectuals." Among the speakers scheduled to sit on panels and interact with one another were George, Said, and a variety of other speakers, from Conor Cruise O'Brien and Leszek Kolakowski to Renata Adler, Jean Elshtain, and Christopher Lasch. Though I assured Said that George would be "alright," I did say that the timing could not have been worse. "That's why I phoned," he answered.

Later that week George arrived, one day before everyone else, and at dinner that evening at our kitchen table he asked if I'd seen Said's review. I had. And yes, I had intended to bring it up. "I don't want to talk about it," George said, "but I simply wanted to be sure you knew."

"But don't you think it's the oddest review you've ever read?" I asked. "I mean, you could mine it for blurbs to include on the backs of all of your books. Sweet revenge, don't you think?"

"I prefer not to think of it," he said, effectively putting an end to the subject—though future editions of George's books did carry excerpts drawn from Said's review.

I awoke the following day with a mild feeling of dread. Peg and I had spent many hours planning this conference, and were obviously excited about what would be said, not to mention the special issue of *Salmagundi* that would be devoted to an edited transcript of the meeting. Several of the other speakers were friends of ours, and I wondered whether they would see to it that things did not get out of hand. Of course, I didn't want George to suffer. Didn't want him to dread these days. He was, as I'd said, a big boy, and he had absorbed attacks before. But those sentences Said had warned me about were personal, not merely nasty but laced with a kind of derision that brought to mind the taunts of schoolboys when they had in their sights another, more vulnerable, boy who inspired in their class or cohort mockery and ridicule. Virtually all of Said's review read like a celebration of George and his work, but the praise did not cancel the targeted and sharply-delivered insult. George would find it hard not to speak of it, and almost impossible to answer. Said and George would be in one another's company for three long days, and participants would look at the two of them and wonder what must be coursing through George's mind as he summoned the stoic countenance he would need to pretend that nothing Said had written could touch him.

At mid-afternoon on Friday, Peg and I drove to the Surrey Inn, directly across from the main entrance of Skidmore College, to greet the speakers, arriving from airports and train stations. Several of our colleagues were there to offer assistance. George had come down from his room and was fully engaged in the inn's grand living room, speaking with other early arrivals. Soon afterwards Said entered, looking characteristically dapper and appealing. He had settled into his room, everything "perfect," and suggested we would talk later. Now he wanted to meet "Steiner" and "get that over with." Was he around? He was. My friend, the novelist Nick Delbanco, would introduce him. And with that Nick steered Said out of the entrance hall and into the far reaches of the cavernous living room, where I watched the "introduction" unfold, from about six feet away, trailing just a bit behind, hoping not to find it necessary to intervene. "George," Nick said, stepping deftly between George and the film critic Stanley Kauffmann, "let me introduce you to Edward Said"—who held out his hand and said, "It's good to meet you at last." To which George said, turning to face Said, "I do not shake hands with scum." Nothing more. Just that.

Said quietly marched away, and said to me, over his retreating shoulder, "Well, that didn't go very well."

"He'll get over it," I said. "Just enjoy your dinner and don't let it spoil your time." Lame, hopelessly lame, I thought, wondering how I might make the situation better. Much better. Though others assured me there was nothing to be done, and that perhaps both George and Edward would perform even better than usual as a result of the animosity that hung, fully charged, in the air we would breathe over the following days.

I don't judge George for what he said to Said. His response was a very human response. Ineffectual. An expression of instinct and barely controlled rage. No doubt George could not adequately appreciate those sentences Said had composed to express his admiration for a thinker he disliked. George's desire was to wound, to preserve his cold fury and to assert his dignity. His sense was that the insult he had received was an attack on his person and thus unforgivable. Though I hoped the admiring paragraphs Said wrote would compensate for the hurt, I understood that the insults had forced George to acknowledge a current of visceral antipathy that was often directed at him.

George spoke at several sessions of the *Salmagundi* conference and never mentioned Edward Said by name. In the audience George sat quietly through a session in which Said's paper on neocolonialism was attacked by Conor Cruise O'Brien and by the historian John Lukacs. Was George thinking about the altercation with Said when he said, at a later session on "The Responsibility of Intellectuals," that "we have the obligation of pressing the unpleasant questions," and that "being so privileged as we are, it is almost our damn job not to ask the nice questions"? But the questions Said had raised at the opening of his review were not only not "nice," but tasteless. And George took the opportunity to speak of Said, without naming him, by noting that there was something indecent about someone who occupied an endowed chair at a major university, enjoying all of the protections and privileges accorded to the holder of such a chair, while inciting violence in the Middle East and never, as it were, putting himself in danger or joining those with whom he professed a spurious solidarity. George might well have been contrasting Said's stance with the stance of Sontag and other intellectuals—Orwell, of course, comes most readily to mind—who had fought or put themselves on the line in one battlefront or another. Said could well have raised his hand and spoken from the floor during that session, in which everyone present knew that George was speaking of him. However, Edward preferred to remain silent, and in a letter to me the following week he complained that he had been badly "outnumbered" at our conference. When I reported Said's grievance to George in a letter, he wrote back to say that Said was never reputed to complain "when he held all the cards" and "no one was present to dispute what he said."

Far and away the most uncomfortable occasions for me were those in which someone I revered unleashed an attack on George. The critic Irving Howe, who had published my first pieces in *Dissent* magazine when I was twenty-two and twenty-three, and written books and essays that seemed to me exemplary, had become a friend, and I was taken aback by his *Harper's Magazine* review of George's book *In Bluebeard's Castle*. The title, "Auschwitz and High Mandarin," will at once suggest its flavor.[61] Throughout the review, Howe exhibited undisguised contempt for the way that George "stimulated himself with high Germanic notions about culture." So turned off was he by George's preening that he did not think it necessary to engage with the thesis of George's polemic. A shame, I felt, in that Irving might well have discovered that he and George saw eye to eye when it came to issues raised in *Bluebeard's Castle*, from the ravages of mass culture to the problem of literacy. But most irritating to Irving were the oracular pronouncements, too many references to "the inhuman potentialities of cultured man" and "penitential ecumenism." And yes, George was excessively given to noting that the gifts of science, the arts, and philosophy "are, will be, to an overwhelming extent, the creation of the gifted few." That emphasis—"the gifted few"—was enough to make Irving lose patience with George, and on that score my sympathies were always with Irving.

I often argued with George about his tendency to come out with statements that made him sound like a man who had not fully considered what might be said against him by critics like Howe. Decidedly, I argued, it is by no means as obvious as George contended that "the very notion of culture [is] tautological with elitism," and in fact George often interjected asides or qualifications that might have pointed the way to a less tendentious statement of his case. He was well aware of an entire tradition of Marxist criticism that regarded art and culture "as instrumentalities of caste and regime." In George's classic essays on Marxist thinkers, there is a counterweight to much that he proposes in *Bluebeard's Castle*, and Howe might have been just the critic to tease out the contradictions.

But Irving was reluctant to seriously engage George on such matters. Moreover, he could not concede that George marshalled his case with remarkable vividness and force, and made palpable and relevant what he most feared in the emergent culture.

Once, in 1990, Irving did concede that the visceral recoil he felt when confronted by "a certain accent or tendency" might best be understood as a matter of disposition and sensibility:

"The differences between us involve a traditional difference of intellectual style," he said, and that would "continue, I suppose, as long as human beings try to think." This was "a difference between, roughly speaking, the Anglo-Saxon, of which I'm a familiar representative, and the Continental."[62]

Here I can't help recalling that, when my long review of George's *After Babel* appeared in the *American Poetry Review* in 1975, Irving told me one afternoon that a mutual friend of ours had sent it to him. Was it alright?

"It sounded like heavy lifting," Irving said. "Not your piece. But the Steiner book. It's a very generous review," he said.

"It's a very brilliant and indispensable book, the best thing Steiner has ever done," I replied.

"I'll take your word for it," Irving said.

4 · MASTER TEACHER

THOSE who knew George were alert to flashes of the peremptory and dismissive tone that crept, very occasionally, into the published work. Often George became angry and disappointed as, for example, on my behalf, when he learned that the circulation of *Salmagundi* magazine—between 4,000 and 5,000 copies—remained that of a "little magazine," and he wondered at my own equanimity in the face of what seemed to him a failure of ambition. Did I not understand that some of the writers I promoted in reviews and essays were "anything but major"? Why waste my time on making the case for them? An odd complaint, in that George frequently advocated for books and writers not well known or widely admired, and both of us believed much was to be said for discovering authors whom others ignored or failed to appreciate.

There were issues, writers, and books George and I simply could not agree upon. Often, when I wrote him about a book I was teaching for the first time, he wrote back wondering why I bothered to share such a work with students who might better have been asked to read something else. In 1993, when I was reading one book after another by Joseph Roth and, for the first time, including him on the syllabus of a graduate course I was teaching at The New School, George wrote to me in a January letter: "*The Radetzky March* is, surely, a poignant and fine book but not a 'great' one. That rubric applies, I hope, to the treatment of these same themes in Musil, in Broch, in parts, even, of Schnitzler." In the first paragraph of that same letter he counters my earlier criticism of a review he had written on J. M. Coetzee's novel *Waiting for the Barbarians*. "I can make no sense," George writes, "of your findings on Coetzee," going on to defend what seemed to me an indefensible argument he had made about the "plagiarism" entailed in Coetzee's borrowings from *The Tartare Steppe* by the Italian novelist Dino Buzzati. Irritated later by what I wrote in praise of Coetzee's *Elizabeth Costello* (2003), *Disgrace* (1999), and his other masterworks, George would occasionally remind me that my assessments were peculiar, even "unreal," as he wrote in a letter of January 1998: "Who will be the next comet in your generous heavens?" he asked, his exasperation there extending even to writers he had admired, from Tzvetan Todorov to Seamus Heaney. "Oh well," he would write, trying hard to strike a more loving and measured tone: "Perhaps your very private and personal 'resurrection'" of selected writers and thinkers "must have its intimate grounds." Yes, I assured him, occasionally there were "intimate grounds," but most often not. "Hope you have HAD A PERFECT and total holiday in Miami," he concludes that lengthy and mainly scornful letter. "And that what comes through to you in this bristly letter is boundless affection and trust."

Though George could hector and complain and contradict, he was most often generous and infectiously gregarious. Even at the seminar table, when I was a graduate student, he seemed to me and to other students anything but drunk on the power he exercised, and though often we were not up to the task, he insistently solicited what he called "collaborative dissent." At a symposium at The New School, after a series of intense but always courteous exchanges on the subject of the "Consciousness Industry," Christopher Hitchens told George, "It's been an honor and an unexpected pleasure to cross swords with you, Professor." Susan Sontag's head may have hurt after spending a few hours with George, but Peg and I spent days on end with him and never found it necessary to resort to aspirin or tranquillizers. In Cambridge, we were invited upstairs to watch with George and his wife, Zara, episodes of the television series *Tinker Tailor Soldier Spy* and afterwards to untangle the narrative. At his best, George was seductively engaging, and even a casual discussion with him was often charged with emotion.

None of the trips we took with George, our dinners in Manhattan, or lunches in Oxford or Cambridge provided a more memorable view of George than the week I spent with him at the University of Geneva, where he had been teaching for many years. Again and again he told me that the real reason I had to come to Geneva was to sit in on his classes—especially the Shakespeare class.

"Why that one?"

"You'll see for yourself," he said. "I don't want to build it up and then have you in any way disappointed. It's not precisely a theatrical event. We spend a semester on a single play. I began several years ago and will continue, semester after semester, until we've read all thirty-seven plays."

"And was this designed for undergraduate students?" I asked.

"You'll see."

George arranged for me to stay at a modest hotel not far from his small apartment. For a long time, he had proposed that I move the family to Geneva and take up a position at the university in his department. He knew that my French was less than rudimentary—"It's actually nonexistent," I would tell him, and then proceed to demonstrate how I couldn't bring out even a single coherent sentence longer than three or four words. But why worry, George insisted. The position he had in mind for me was in English studies, where I would lecture in English. Yes, yes, it would be awkward for a while, not being able to converse comfortably with colleagues whose English was as poor as my French. But how long could it take for me to master a language I would hear every day? I reminded him that his brilliant wife, Zara, a distinguished historian, was for the most part as monolingual as I was, although both of us could read—with some difficulty—other languages. Like me, Zara was married to someone who was fabulously good at picking up new languages, and fearless in trying them out. George couldn't quite accept that other educated beings, Americans especially, might have reason for anxiety about language acquisition.

Tempting though the prospect of moving to Geneva was, I soon came to think it all impossible. Not for Peg and me. Not even with an offer from the university to take over publication of *Salmagundi* magazine. Had I been able to imagine building the kind of following George had attracted, no doubt I might well have been more ambivalent. But no one—absolutely no one—had attracted the following I observed in George's weekly two-and-a-half-hour Shakespeare class. I met briefly at 9:00 a.m. with two of George's graduate students, who escorted me to reserved seating in a large auditorium already filled to capacity. Well over six hundred people assembled every Wednesday morning to work on a Shakespeare play, though fewer than thirty were enrolled in the course for academic credit. Another fifty or so were nonmatriculated students at the university. The others—as I was soon to learn at a reception—were assorted academics, politicians, lawyers, physicians, poets, and business people. As I scanned the room I saw that each held in hand the

Robert Boyers, Zara Steiner, and George Steiner at the Steiner house on Barrow Road, Cambridge, England, 1979.

George Steiner and Robert Boyers at the Boyers house in Saratoga Springs, 1986.

Shaul Bakhash, George Steiner, and Susan Sontag at the *Salmagundi* "Race, Religion & Nationalism" conference, Skidmore College, 1989.

Erich Heller at the Boyers house, Saratoga Springs, 1983.

Robert Boyers, Leszek Kolakowski, and George Steiner at the *Salmagundi*
"Intellectuals" conference, Skidmore College, 1985.

Leszek Kolakowski and Peg Boyers at the *Salmagundi* "Intellectuals" conference, Skidmore College, 1985.

George Steiner and Conor Cruise O'Brien at the *Salmagundi* "Intellectuals" conference, Skidmore College, 1985.

Edward Said at
Columbia University,
2000.

Kwame Anthony Appiah at the *Salmagundi* "Race, Religion and
Nationalism" conference, 1989.

David Steiner and David Rieff at the *Salmagundi* "Race Religion, and Nationalism" conference, Skidmore College, 1989.

J. M. Coetzee and Robert Boyers at the Boyers house, Saratoga Springs, 1996.

same compact edition of *Othello*. George had arrived at the lectern by the time I entered, and was engaged in conversation with two colleagues, waiting for the 9:30 start time for the class. I expected from George a lecture to kick things off, but when we began it became clear this was not to be an occasion for lecturing. Though he was the most thrilling lecturer I had ever witnessed, and he knew that his reputation as a lecturer had attracted much of the audience, he was determined not to deliver the very thing that would have seemed most predictable for an enormous audience spread across a large auditorium. Of course, George didn't need to deliver a formal lecture to deploy his rhetorical gifts and to use his voice as an instrument of considerable range and surprising effects.

In any case, George had decided to handle the Shakespeare class somewhat in the way he organized a much smaller Tuesday afternoon class in literary theory. The approach, a combination of close reading and encounter, offered students—all six hundred and more of them—face to face exchange. Honest teaching, in George's sense of what that meant, entailed a spirited process in which amendment and rebuttal, questions and objections, were at least possible, the student attentive and thus answerable, poised to respond even if, in that auditorium, only a handful of responses might be summoned. With *Othello* open in his hand, George led us through a small portion of the text, reading aloud, pausing over particular words or phrases, questioning his own take on an anomaly or apparent obscurity in the language. Throughout, I could sense that each person in the room felt nothing could be more important than the close readings we had been strenuously invited to perform. Hands went up, students spoke, some from the far reaches of the auditorium.

Only years later, in 2002, after hearing George's *Lessons of the Masters* lectures at Harvard, did I have the language—George's language—adequate to capture the felt power of this experience: "A Master invades, he breaks open," George wrote in those lectures, and he did surely break open each person in that Geneva auditorium; he opened us to intensities of feeling and even uncomfortable thoughts that would at once seem indispensable.[63] Above all, he elicted from each of us an uncommon degree of attention, and communicated the sense that we were not mere onlookers at a spectacle belonging only to certified masters, or to the tradition, or to academic scholarship. No one in that auditorium felt remote from the work we were called to do. Here was a community devoted to an exercise in sheer pleasurable, unremitting exertion. Often that exertion was applied to the unriddling of sentences, the savoring of improbable locutions, the leap from the text before us to another that would provide further illumination. George's persistent "you will recall" in this setting was a summons to his hundreds of "regulars" in that audience to remember other semesters in which they had studied together *Lear* or *Hamlet* or *Twelfth Night*.

"Is this a moment," George asked, "when Othello betrays an inner being? Is it our conviction that we are throughout in touch with that inner being?" To which first one woman, then another, responded by recalling George's sessions on *Hamlet* a year earlier, when they had concluded that the prince himself shows only an opaque and impenetrable surface. "Whereas with Othello," said the older woman, "you never feel there is within him merely a void, a nothing, that he masks his inner being as Hamlet does."

This exchange, in turn, led George to further juxtapose the two plays, the two characters. "Is it not the case," he asked, "that for Hamlet the women have no human reality, that for him both Ophelia and Gertrude are in effect private symbols for his own detestation of the world—whereas one can say no such thing about Othello's relation to Desdemona, who enjoys a symbolic status, certainly, and yet is very much for her husband a flesh and blood reality." To have no sense of that difference, as between the one character and the other in their respective views of the women in their lives, was to miss an essential component of both plays.

Also striking was George's summons to us to consider whether in *Othello* there was a place for joy. Was it fair to say that even in this work the darkness is not absolute? Might we together identify in the text, somewhere, a pulse of humor or lightness? In *The Death of Tragedy*, George said, he wanted to suggest that, however unrelenting the darkness, there is in tragedy some prospect of alleviation, or if not that, then at least recompense. And if that might be so, where, he asked, would that be found, here, in the work before us? Might it be here, in this passage—which he read aloud—or in this one? He was not thinking merely that a character like Cassio would go on to govern Cyprus more efficiently than Othello. That was not the recompense George would have us consider. And so, what then? An instigation fruitfully and gratefully met by each of us.

In Geneva, I was experiencing a George Steiner who had grown enormously in the quarter century since I first studied with him in New York. Improbably, given the size of the Geneva audience, he taught as one who thought himself both learner and messenger, scholarly exemplar and friend. In the Norton Lectures he wrote of the exchange that occurs in a genuine pedagogic encounter as "an eros of reciprocal trust and, indeed, love," so that "the intensity of the dialogue generates friendship in the highest sense," and in remembering that unforgettable morning in Geneva, I think I understood what George intended in resorting to those improbably exalted and yet intimate words.

The trust and the courage were evident in the candid and searching comments or questions called out by at least a dozen students. To my surprise, I saw in George's responses and solicitations that he came across as a maestro, companionable and yet exigent, the willing servant of a text he took to be the vehicle for communicating insights and sensations indispensable to himself and to us. Moving about the lectern, standing away from it and often looking out and up, meeting our eyes, he was clearly someone for whom everything that transpired was deeply personal. His avidity was palpable and irresistible. His unpacking of the text had not the slightest trace of pedantry. This Master wanted not disciples but a wide circle of communicants sharing their not-so-secret passion in what felt like a sacred space.

At the reception that followed the morning session I spoke with a good many people. A handful were students I'd seen the day before at George's Tuesday seminar. But most of those I met were older—age range forty to sixty, one or two older—many of them traveling to Geneva each week expressly to attend George's Shakespeare class. Some flew in or took the train from Paris or Milan and cities in other European countries, settling in at their Geneva hotels on Tuesday evenings and planning to return to their home countries that evening or later in the week. Several spoke of having attended the Shakespeare sessions for a decade and of hoping to persist through all thirty-seven plays. They were knowledgeable about their teacher's work and thought him the ideal instructor. Though most had known Steiner only in this one setting, they thought of him as a comrade-in-arms, a partner in an enterprise they would not

have undertaken without him. An older man, a Parisian, introduced himself to me as a corporate lawyer who had always
wanted to return to the study of Shakespeare and found in
George a teacher who made him feel at last adequate to the
task. Nothing in this, the lawyer said, to make you feel superflu-
ous, that there are the real scholars like Steiner himself and
then, on the other side, the lumpen types whose views and
insights no one would care to solicit. No, this was, so the lawyer
and others told me, as close to an ideal community of learners
as they could imagine.

At lunch afterwards, with perhaps twenty of us at the table,
I found myself addressed now and then in French, and thus
several times having to make my apologies, with George then
apologizing for me by assuring our companions that, in addition to English, I was more than competent in other European
languages. So that I spent much of the time worrying that
someone at the table would expect to carry on with me a lively
conversation in one of those other European languages—Italian and Spanish—in which I would at once prove myself, to say
the least, disappointing.

My good fortune was that a middle-aged woman seated
across from me, in a booming voice, mentioned (in English,
thank heavens), that she had been struck by my defense of
George's controversial Hitler novel, *The Portage to San Cristobal
of A. H.*, in *Atrocity and Amnesia*, my recent book on the politics
of novels and novelists. In fact, she said that the Steiner chapter
was the only one in my book that she had found "bizarre."
"Granted it was clever," she went on, "and I imagine your
friend George was grateful, and yet, you can't actually expect
anyone to believe that the words spoken by A. H. in that novel
belong to anyone but George Steiner himself. I mean," she
said, "can anyone imagine the Führer describing the master

race as 'a parody—a hungry imitation' of the Jewish idea of the Chosen people?"

"I'm impressed," I said, "that you have the words of the novel by heart."

"Five words, at any rate," she said, "maybe a few more. But I read your chapter only recently, and when I heard from George that you were to be here I thought I'd ask. Politely."

Some nervous laughter then around the table. Laughter at the way my interlocutor had commandeered the table and put George's visitor somewhat on the spot. Perhaps also some amusement at the way that George had clearly decided to stay out of it, as if he were only as interested and involved as the others seated there. His conviction, certainly, that a question, or challenge, put to me in perfectly lucid English I could well take on all by myself, as in fact I could.

I hated having to respond to questions at a lunch table in a teacherly way. And much that I was called upon to say seemed to me almost too obvious to bother about. That George's novel had a lot to do with language subversion, rhetorical sleight of hand, and appropriation, a procedure that Adolph Hitler, as well as Steiner's A. H. character, had brought to perfection.

"And so you actually believe," my antagonist persisted, "that Hitler was capable of using words such as those your friend puts in his mouth?"

"If the novel doesn't make you believe it, then of course you won't believe it," I said.

Was George a great novelist? By no means. Nor was I required, in Geneva or anywhere else, to argue that he was. In his *Paris Review* interview he makes it perfectly clear that he does not regard himself as a creative writer to set beside those who matter. Not even beside those, like Arthur Koestler or André Malraux, for whom arguments and ideas play an outsize role in their fiction. But the attacks on *The Portage* were of a piece with others leveled at George, in that they often seemed willfully obtuse, as if intended to discredit not what he had actually written but to impugn his motives. When *The Portage* appeared, several notices were clearly inspired by a loathing for what George had written elsewhere, particularly about Israel as a nation state armed to the teeth and driven by ambitions all too reflective of a militant and belligerent nationalism. And thus George's novel was felt by many to be of a piece with the tendency to strike a posture unbecoming to a Jewish intellectual of his generation and background. How dare he give the last word in the novel to A. H.? Was this not proof positive that George was an irresponsible provocateur, and perhaps something worse?

Not all critics of the novel agreed that it was merely a provocation. Adam Gopnik later wrote in the the *New Yorker* that George's "study of language, *After Babel*, and his daunting but in its way astounding novel *The Portage to San Cristobal of A. H.* are perhaps the likeliest to go on being read, or at least remembered."[64] George would not have agreed with Gopnik's prediction for *The Portage*, though he hoped that at least the two long speeches in the novel, one delivered by Hitler himself, the other by the Nazi hunter Lieber who tracks him down, would continue to seem compelling.

At the Geneva lunch table another of George's colleagues asked whether in publishing his essay "Our Homeland, the Text" in *Salmagundi*, I had been persuaded by his assertion that the true homeland of the Jew is "the text," and that in reality the fate of the Jews, and their inalienable gift, has always been to live without a homeland.

"Never sure," I replied, "that I can go all the way with George on that issue, but then I can never again think about the fate of the Jews without his thesis in mind."

"So you're not persuaded, though you like the ring of it," said the man.

"Well," I said, "I'm persuaded by what George says of nationalism. Forgive me, but I can quote a key sentence, to the effect that 'the man or woman at home in the text is, by definition, a conscientious objector: to the vulgar mystique of the flag and the anthem, to the sleep of reason which proclaims "my country right or wrong."' "Does that sound about right, George," I asked? A head nod from George. A sly lifting of the eyebrow. Nothing more.

And though old arguments about *The Portage* are perhaps not worth joining again, I never took seriously the charge that in his writings on Jewishness and Zionism George exhibited a willful, even perverse, refusal of solidarity with his own people. The same kind of charge was directed at Hannah Arendt by Gershom Scholem and other critics, who claimed that Arendt did not sufficiently demonstrate in her work a fitting love for her people. That she was disloyal. As for George, and for Arendt and Sontag as well, parochial claims of disloyalty could only seem petty and irrelevant. He understood that the demands of scholarship, like the claims of the creative imagination, must often lead writers to places apt to seem intolerable and out of bounds to some of their readers. Though George never laid claim to the indisputable rightness of his ideas nor to the certainty of their eventual acceptance, he was willing always to do what Elias Canetti demanded of the true writer: "to stick his damp nose into everything."

5 · AN EVENING WITH ARTHUR KOESTLER

T HOUGH I wrote quite often about George's work, I did not invariably approve of what he'd written, and occasionally conceded to his critics more than he thought I should. Invited to speak at a Nexus symposium in The Netherlands in 2000, George delivered the keynote lecture, "Farewell to the Muses." I was stirred by what he said and yet filled with misgivings. I knew that George would expect nothing less than an honest airing of our differences, and when I returned to the United States I laid out my misgivings in a long letter. At dinner after his lecture he had proposed that I publish the text in *Salmagundi*, and I thought it necessary to include among my misgivings the fact that certain aspects of his argument were familiar to me, and had in fact appeared in another essay of his that we had published two or three years earlier. He bristled at the suggestion that he had repeated himself, but when I told him that I would publish his new essay and respond at length to it in a piece of my own, he welcomed the prospect.

"Would you wish to have the last word?"

"Not necessary," he said. "I'll say what I have to say, and you will answer."

George's lecture was characteristically eloquent and impressive in marshalling a vast range of sources—from Pindar to Schiller, from Condorcet to Mahler and Wittgenstein. He argued that artists and thinkers have long understood that "humanism" is "powerless" in the face of bestiality. "Each epoch," George observed, "has claimed to hear the muses' adieu, the still sad music of the departing Hercules in *Antony and Cleopatra* or the collective exit of the gods, of the divine which is the leitmotif in Hölderlin." The sense of decline he anatomized led on to the observation that cultivated literacy is no bar to murder and mayhem. That great artists and writers have often been accomplices to brutality, or scandalously indifferent. The belief that the spread of education might change society for the better is clearly not supported—so he contended—by the historical record. The immersion in Shakespeare, the capacity to be moved by a demanding poem or a Schubert lieder may diminish our capacity to hear "the cry in the street."

Though I had confronted these observations before in several of George's lectures and books, I was never quite certain what to do with them. I knew that a good many readers were hungry for confirmation that the humanities fail to humanize. Others questioned or derided George's sense that we needed to be reminded of something they thought obvious. George was well aware that numerous thinkers had engaged with the fact that we live in a post-theological age, that many of us have learned to live without recourse to god terms. Others had asked whether there can be "major art, literature, music and metaphysics" under such conditions. But when George raised this question, he frequently stirred something less than respectful disagreement. "The death of the Author having been announced several years ago in France," Salman Rushdie wrote, "and the death of Tragedy by Professor Steiner himself in an earlier obituary—that leaves the stage strewn with more bodies than the end of *Hamlet*."[65]

The argument I chose to pick with George had principally to do with his capitulation to an agenda dictated by facts and portents that seemed to me not quite to add up. I suggested that he was perhaps unduly awed by what he took to be the prevailing signs of decline, to read into them large meanings and predictive patterns. Was it true, as George wished us to believe, that the vitality of a culture is best measured by the masterpieces produced under its auspices, or—much more important—that a prevailing sense of living in what Ezra Pound called "a botched civilization" will doom other artists and thinkers to mediocrity? Was it not true that when Matthew Arnold spoke of "anarchy and decline," a hundred and fifty years earlier, European culture was entering a period of extraordinary vitality, when the novels of Stendhal and Flaubert, Dickens and George Eliot were already in the air he breathed? Did not Spengler in 1920 write of the decline of the West when Mann and Proust, Joyce and Woolf, Kafka and Italo Svevo were creating permanent works of unsurpassable vitality nourished by the very idea of decline and fall they explored in their supreme fictions?

There was more to my argument, and when we sat together at breakfast one morning in Tilburg, he acknowledged one point at least: that temperament determines, to a considerable degree, our inclinations to read the available portents in one way rather than another. As an American, George said, you're bound to be an optimist. That is a given of your own disposition. To which I could only reply that he was again setting in place a kind of determinism. I was bound to be . . . I was an American who must therefore be predisposed to . . . These formulas, I said, really do go to the heart of our differences.

After all, I'm an American who studied with George Steiner and Conor Cruise O'Brien. Who teaches *After Babel* and *Language and Silence.* Temperament matters, yes, and I was grateful to George for conceding that much in his response to my paper "A Refusal to Mourn the Death of the Muses." But the recourse to "temperament" could only be a preliminary suggestion. I would not allow that my inveterate optimism, such as it was, had blinded me to reality. And neither would I allow that George saw only what he was determined to see. My view was not fatally constrained by my being an American. Neither was George utterly constrained by his being, as he once wrote, "a kind of survivor" of the Holocaust. That fact was a constitutive aspect of his very being and definitively influenced his outlook, but it did not prevent him from tasting all too human pleasures.

Often I remarked to George that he actually liked to be argued with. Frequently there was mischief in the way he answered a challenge, claiming for his own position what was certain to lead to further opposition. One evening in the spring of 1980 Peg and I had dinner with the Steiners in their Cambridge house on Barrow Road when the other guests were Arthur Koestler and his wife, Cynthia. Several years earlier, I had published in the *New Republic* a somewhat querulous review of Koestler's *The Heel of Achilles*, and wondered whether he would have read it, or cared. For his part, George had approved of my review, and asked that just this once I should keep this to myself. Koestler was reputed to be somewhat of a brawler, who had been involved in fistfights with Camus and Sartre, among others. But George thought Koestler, at this late stage of his life, rather a changed man, and not much given to anger or controversy. A man with Parkinson's, who used a cane and moved cautiously. I had long admired Koestler's *Darkness at Noon*, and I was more than a little pleased to be spending an evening with him.

Koestler was, after all, a man who had fought in the great European conflicts of the twentieth century and witnessed political sordidness far removed from my modest experience of political struggle. George thought Koestler had exerted a beneficial influence on Orwell, who admired him, though Koestler's well-documented swings from one form of zealotry to another always made him a less reliably sober witness than Orwell. Was it possible, George asked me in the hour before the Koestlers arrived, that a man who could write with such cunning and precision about the Communist mind—a mind he knew, as it were, from the inside—could have visited the Soviet Union in the early thirties and seen nothing disturbing, and then gone to Spain during the civil war as an agent of the Comintern? It was possible. True, Koestler's experience of Spain rapidly turned him around, so that in the 1940s he would contribute an essay to *The God That Failed*, an immensely consequential volume that collected the writings of other disillusioned former Communists, including Richard Wright, Andre Gide, and Ignazio Silone. But Koestler went on in later years to invest in several dubious theories—political, religious, anthropological, scientific—and George was not averse to asking him questions that were bound to be provocative.

From the moment Koestler arrived I saw that he and George knew each other quite well. They had played chess together, and each spoke with some avidity of people and issues they'd discussed before. I was slow to jump in, but when I asked Koestler what he was working on he asked me—in perfect English, but with a decided Middle-European accent—whether I "followed" his recent work.

"I'm most familiar with your earlier books, like *Darkness at Noon*," I said, "and the essays in *The Yogi and the Commissar*."

"What do you admire in the essays?" Koestler asked, standing for the moment just a bit closer to me than I would have liked. "Not too dark for a young American like you?"

"Robert has been trying to make himself into a European intellectual for at least ten or fifteen years," George intervened, "though I've told him it's hopeless."

"I like dark," I said, trying to be confident and clever but sounding, certainly to myself, glib and foolish.

"What else do you like, apart from dark?" Koestler asked.

"I like knowing that the man interrogating me was once a disciplined revolutionary who found a way to assert his independence."

"And you know, then, what independence means?" asked Koestler, looking over at George with an expression that seemed to say, Who is this pathetic American?

"Well, since you ask what I like," I said, "I'll tell you that I don't much like being interrogated, not even by Arthur Koestler."

"Perhaps you'd prefer instead to interrogate me," he said.

"You'll let him do that another time," George said.

"Don't be a bore," Koestler shot back.

"The first time," I said, "that anyone has ever called George Steiner a bore."

"He's heard a lot worse," Koestler said, without a smile. "Even from me."

When Peg and I got back to our rooms at Churchill College that night I sat up for almost two hours writing out what I could recall of the exchanges I'd witnessed. George had stirred Koestler by telling him that some years ago I'd published a short book about Lionel Trilling, knowing very well that Koestler had little fondness for Trilling.

"That man played it safe," Koestler said. "He stayed out of trouble, which isn't much of a recommendation. And I don't think I'll read your book."

"That would be a mistake," George said.

I'd never heard George speak well of Trilling before, but he was clearly impatient with Koestler's breezily dismissive tone, and soon found himself extolling Trilling's resistance to simple or stark dualisms. "He gave a good name to moderation," George said.

"Is this Steiner I'm hearing?" Koestler asked. "Is this the man who condescends to intellectuals who blow neither hot nor cold? To trimmers? I thought I was dining with a fire breather, and here I'm seated across from . . . someone else. Next thing," he said, "you'll be using words like nobility and other rotten expressions."

At one point in the evening Koestler asked if George had spoken to me or Peg about the bad time he'd had at Cambridge years earlier. "He doesn't like to talk about it," Koestler said, "but it's left a scar."

"I like to think I got over it, long ago," George said. "But I imagine it's with me still, somewhere."

At which I reminded George that the first letters I had sent him, decades earlier, were addressed to Professor George Steiner at Churchill College, so that he had to inform me that he was not at that time a professor, and I was not to post letters to the Churchill College address using that title. A long and unhappy story, he wrote to me, promising to fill in the details at some future time. Which he did one rainy afternoon when we were seated together in the Kings College office of Frank Kermode, who had just recently been through his own miserable time at Cambridge and knew first-hand what academic politics and bad faith might amount to.

As an occasional visitor to Cambridge in the 1980s and in

subsequent decades, with no previous experience of Oxbridge life, I found it hard to imagine the atmosphere of late sixties and early seventies conflict, when the barbs were flying and accusations of antisemitism were very much in the Cambridge air. By the time I arrived there George was teaching for part of each year in Geneva, though he and Zara lived much of the year in Cambridge on a bucolic street in a fine though by no means grand brick house. They had friends at the university, and enjoyed what such a place offered. They had their favorite pubs and nearby country inns, attended public lectures at the different colleges, extolled the virtues of the Fitzwilliam Museum, and gave occasional dinner parties at the house. When George was at home they enjoyed a weekly high table dinner with the other Fellows at Churchill College, where George was "Extraordinary Fellow" and had college rooms at his disposal. From time to time he would stroll into the comfortable Fellows reading room and peruse the international newspapers and periodicals, and when I joined him there I saw that he was not uneasy in that setting, however much the Cambridge scene remained for him the site of his early disappointment.

That disappointment arose from the fact that George was never offered a professorial or university appointment, in spite of his enormous following as a lecturer at Churchill College and his fame as a scholar and writer. For many in the Cambridge scene this was a scandal, and it was much discussed in common rooms and written up in the English newspapers. Had George made it clear that he regarded much that transpired in the humanities at Cambridge as narrow and provincial? He had. Did he routinely deride the tendency among English literary academics to limit their researches and their curricula to English language works and to exclude from the curriculum the study of comparative literature? He did. Was it not his practice to challenge the academic status quo by insisting that his literature students become fully conversant with the works of Marx, Freud, Levi-Strauss, and other thinkers like George Lukacs and Walter Benjamin?

It was. So that it cannot have been surprising to learn that, among some of those who might have been moved to confer a professorial appointment, George seemed the wrong sort of fellow. That he was regarded as "unclubbable" and "foreign" was often remarked, and such epithets appeared in stories about the Steiner affair at Cambridge.

Such epithets always struck me as anything but innocent, and I wondered what lay behind a little joke I heard one evening at a dinner with the critic Erich Heller, who told me that in English academic circles George was frequently referred to as "the Jewish Isaiah Berlin." Comic, to be sure, and yet troubling, as Heller himself agreed. Berlin was a Jewish intellectual, but one who had charmed his British hosts at Oxford and in the larger British political establishment. He was an independent thinker whose views were sensible and reliably liberal. Like George a great talker, Berlin managed not to provoke or offend. Like others in his cohort, he thought George electric and brilliant, but also too much. Even George's learning he thought extravagant—extravagant in the way it was paraded. Though Berlin would not have said so quite so baldly, George clearly seemed to him to call too much attention to his passions, his unorthodox ideas, his obsession with the Holocaust and with Jewish writers and thinkers. To those for whom George was "the Jewish Isaiah Berlin," he was somehow unassimilable, never quite "our kind," always uncomfortably "foreign." His tendency to work outwards from particular literary instances to what he called "the far reaches of moral and political argument" seemed to his detractors a fault, an over-reaching, and unbecoming to one who wished to hold a secure position in an established community of moderate strivers.

At our dinner together Koestler referred to George's "naughty" tendency to come out with assertions that would surely unsettle his hosts, and recalled that, in his T. S. Eliot Memorial lectures, he admonished Eliot for neglecting to address the implications of the Holocaust in a book (*Notes Towards the Definition of Culture*), published just three years after the end of the war. "You are annoying, George," Koestler said. "No wonder they didn't want you around." Also there was, I suggested, more than a little discomfort with the fact that Steiner was always pressing upon his students works by the great Jewish thinkers, claiming that many of the shaping ideas of modernity were in large measure the creation of these Jewish thinkers. Though we didn't have with us the text of an article by John Carroll, a prominent academic insider who witnessed the hostilities unleashed at Cambridge in the years before George became at last a permanent professor of English and Comparative Literature at the University of Geneva, Koestler alluded to Carroll's essay on the scandal. On the following day George brought it with him to lunch, and together we read the following sentences: "The presence of a central European Jew as fluent in German, French and Italian as in English is not only alien in this provincial country town but also threatening. There is a power in his vast erudition and culture which appears to have made some of those who have confined their interest to the English tradition uncomfortable."[66]

At lunch the next day George also thanked me for providing the occasion—I would have called it the target—that had brought Koestler out of what had become his customary diffidence. No sign, George said, of the depression that has overtaken him. Good that you got to see him as he was last night, George went on, recalling a number of unforgettable sentences that had suddenly erupted in the course of our conversation, when Koestler spoke of his childhood, growing up on the shores of the Danube, and how he had always felt sorry for towns without a river or bridges. A city without bridges, Koestler had said, is like a woman without a necklace or adornments.

6 · "A BRAVE BEGINNING"

ALMOST a year after our week in Cambridge, Peg and I arranged to meet George in Manhattan during his annual spring visit, when he spent time at the *New Yorker* offices selecting books to review. He was eager to talk about the books and the essays he planned to write about them. Already he'd had a long run at the *New Yorker*, and still he was grateful for the freedom he had to write at unusual length when the spirit moved him. One night at George's favorite Manhattan restaurant, The Copenhagen, in Midtown, George surprised us by suggesting that we devote an issue of *Salmagundi* to the subject of homosexuality. This was in the spring of 1981, at least a year before AIDS became front page news. George had remarked numbers of times that a considerable proportion of the artists and writers, dancers and composers he admired were gay. We talked about gay intellectuals in our own circles, whose style and brilliance seemed to George to bespeak a sensibility that differed from anything he associated with less original writers or thinkers. I reminded him that many "straight" writers were equally playful and unorthodox in striking ways. But George would say that we don't know about any of this, about the open frontier between body and soul, where important questions lie. Questions bearing upon the vagaries of libidinal contact and gratification, the relation between biology and culture. Once he had laid out a proposal and committed himself to writing a preface to the prospective volume, I felt it impossible not to proceed.

As it happened, I had ample contacts with many of the writers who came immediately to mind, virtually all of whom leapt at the opportunity to contribute to the special issue we were planning. Several had written for the magazine on other subjects, among them historians like Martin Duberman, John Boswell, Paul Robinson, and George Chauncey, the sociologists Philip Rieff and Peter Sedgwick, and an assortment of literary critics and scholars, including Jill Johnston, Robert Alter, Catherine Stimpson, and Calvin Bedient. George was delighted that Michel Foucault had agreed to sit for a long interview at his Paris apartment, to be conducted by Peg's brother, James O'Higgins, who had written a thesis on Foucault at Louvain and gladly accepted the assignment to fly from New York. George and I agreed that several of the pieces we commissioned would have to be first-person, memoiristic essays, and in the end we regarded the volume as a brave beginning. Of course we could not know that within a year of publication, in late November 1982, our special issue would soon seem out of touch with the immediate reality of AIDS, which suddenly dominated every consideration in the precinct we had hoped to explore.

We also didn't anticipate how controversial this issue of *Salmagundi* would become. George and I had selected contributors diverse enough to ensure the conversations would be anything but ideologically one-dimensional. A number of the twenty essays were opinionated and argumentative, as we had hoped. As they came in and I mailed the more problematic ones to George for comment, we proposed adjustments here and there. George felt the volume would provide at least a "discarded preface" to what would someday be "the 'great book' on homoeroticism, culture, and society."[67]

In a letter of December 1982, George reported that the *Salmagundi* issue had reached him in England, at last. "Privileged and proud to see our names linked," he wrote: "There is genius," he continues, "in your vision of *Salmagundi*, and I do not use such a word often or lightly." Of course he went on, in the same letter, to cite the mistranslations from the French in an otherwise "absorbing" essay on Daniel Guerin, and to complain of a few "pedestrian" essays we'd agreed to include, which didn't quite seem to me pedestrian.

No surprise that George's initial "awe" and enthusiasm would soon sour, so that in a letter of January 1983, only a month later, he would lament "an emptiness of response to the homosexuality issue—which really has god's plenty in it to debate and deepen. Am I really wrong when I sense the echoless, consuming nature of non-events in the American life of the mind?" For George, this "echoless" situation was to be contrasted with the "European densities of resonance and criticism."

But George's disappointment about the apparent silence that greeted our issue was premature. I had told him on another occasion that it was foolish to expect the mainstream press to devote reviews to any little magazine, in spite of the fact that now and again *Salmagundi* did inspire commentary in the pages of the *Village Voice*, the *New York Times* and other publications. And really, as it turned out, there was nothing "empty" about the reception of our volume on homosexuality, however disappointing and, in some respects, predictable were aspects of that reception. The good news was that the Foucault interview was at once regarded as a document of significance, in which a major thinker spoke frankly about matters he had not previously been so open about. Within a month of publication we were flooded with requests for translation rights from magazines all over the world, and that was true to a lesser extent for other essays in the issue. No brief excerpts can fully indicate the richness of Foucault's remarks, but here, in any case, are a few:

> For a homosexual the best moment of love is likely to be when the lover leaves in the taxi. It is when the act is over and the boy is gone that one begins to dream about the warmth of his body, the quality of his smile, the tone of his voice.

> The modern homosexual experience has no relation at all to courtship. . . . [I]n western Christian culture homosexuality was banished and therefore had to concentrate all its energy on the act of sex itself. . . . The wink on the street, the split-second decision to get it on, the speed with which homosexual relations are consummated: all these are products of an interdiction.

> A whole new art of sexual practice develops which tries to explore all the internal possibilities of sexual conduct. You find emerging in places like San Francisco and New York what might be called laboratories of sexual experimentation. You might look upon this as the counterpart of the medieval courts where strict rules of proprietary courtship were defined.[68]

Such observations were of a piece with the perspectives expressed by other contributors to the volume, but Foucault's enormous influence and authority among American intellectuals made the interview a document of the first importance for many readers.

Other features of the volume were provocative in quite different ways. Jill Johnston wrote of "grafting 'lesbian' and 'feminist' together indelibly on the public imagination," even as "feminists in the meantime were ever quietly busy discrediting lesbians, purging their cause of its embarrassing element, the element they felt would most likely frighten off women who might otherwise join the movement."[69] Paul Robinson offered advice and encouragement to a young man struggling to come out, working through "romantic" ideas about the relation between sex and love and insisting that, whatever he says about sexual freedom, "I'm just not going to let sex rule me, as I sense it rules so many people."[70] Arno Karlen wrote of the "new lesbian politics" and asked why many lesbians believed "gay men are like straight men in that they couldn't give a fuck about women."[71] In an essay on Proust and homosexuality, Robert Alter studied the way that many scholars willfully misrepresent sexuality, treating it "as a matter of taste, preference, or inclination," thereby equating sexuality with "coffee-drinking, smoking, chess-playing": "All connections between sexuality and the unconscious are in this fashion brushed aside," and representations of sexuality we find in Shakespeare, Joyce, or Proust—"in which man's sexual urge is seen as imperious, overpowering, rooted in a chthonic realm of fantasies and fears and dreams"— are entirely ignored or misread.[72]

Many readers—to judge from the letters we received—were much taken with the individual case histories on Wittgenstein, Whitman, Wilde, and Proust, and these were often cited in academic books over the next decade. The scholarly essays— by George Chauncey on female deviance and by John Boswell on the history of attitudes towards homosexuality—were quickly translated into other languages and included in anthologies. The first-person memoirs by Martin Bauml Duberman, Jill Johnston, and Paul Robinson provided an access into concerns and practices with which readers had scant familiarity. Other essays, though obviously bracing and pertinent, were felt to be "disturbing." George predicted, in a trans-Atlantic phone call, that the essay by Larry Nachman on Jean Genet would arouse anger. While he felt the profile of Genet was entirely accurate, it was also marked by a moralism that would seem misplaced. Nachman focused on what he took to be Genet's conversion of men to what he called "mere instruments," and went so far as to note that this was something "against which Kant warned and which totalitarian regimes attempt to realize." What Nachman wrote, George said, will seem to many of our readers "distasteful." That was the risk.

One objection to our volume seemed to us bizarre, and seems so still. It was voiced at a special meeting of the Modern Language Association, by assorted academics as well as a few who had contributed to the issue. This pertained to the makeup of our contributors' roster. Why, it was asked, were there so few gay writers represented? Wasn't it obvious that the validity of such a volume had everything to do with the weight accorded in it to the voices of those who knew best what homosexuality entailed?

George heard of this objection even before I did, and when we spoke about it he asked me whether in fact there was anything to be said for the charge simply in statistical terms. He knew that several prominent writers were speaking in the first person about themselves and that I had asked them to do so not only because they were superb writers but because they had written previously about their own gay experience. But what of the others? Could it be, George asked, that there were no other gay writers who had been invited to contribute? And was this a failure or dereliction on our part—principally on my part?

As I told George, I had not thought to wonder in every case whether a contributor was or was not gay. I had never met the literary scholar Robert Alter, whose work I had published earlier in *Salmagundi* and whose wide-ranging literary essays and books I admired. He had mentioned in a letter that he was thinking of writing an essay on Proust, and I had no reason to doubt that he would write brilliantly on Proust and homosexuality. Similarly, I had published essays by Calvin Bedient, knew him to be a first-rate scholar and poetry critic and did not doubt that he'd have much to say about Whitman. Did I know if Alter and Bedient were gay? In 1981 it would not have seemed to me necessary to ask them. If the essays they produced seemed to George or to me anything but cogent and informative we'd have rejected them, as we did in fact reject several pieces we'd commissioned. Was there reason to suppose that only a gay writer could conceivably do justice to Proust or Whitman? The question seems to me now offensive and ridiculous, though it is just the sort of question that continues now to exercise many literary academics.

As it happens, ten of the twenty contributors we had assembled for our issue were indeed gay, and their writing constitutes more than half the pages in the *Salmagundi* issue. Is that enough? Again, the question itself would seem important only if the volume did not clearly feature a number of articles by prominent gay writers, and if the essays by others like Alter or Calvin Bedient betrayed a disabling ideological bias or blindness.

When Peg and I next saw George in New York, he asked about one contributor, Willard Spiegelman, who had written on gay journalism. Did I know him personally? George wanted to know. I did. And did I agree that it was impossible to say, on the basis of the essay he'd written, whether he was or was not a gay intellectual? Agreed, I said, though he'd spoken with me about the gay press, and I knew of his interest in the subject— again, it did not occur to me to ask him whether his interest in the subject had anything to do with his being a gay man. Neither did Willard ever come out to me in our few encounters, even when he invited me to lecture at Southern Methodist University in Dallas. And so it was not obvious to you, one way or another, George asked, that Spiegelman was gay? I knew that he was, I said, or thought I knew, but we spoke always of other things, and I wanted to respect what I took to be his desire not to discuss his sexuality.

Our close friends included gay people who spoke openly of their sexual proclivities, and others who did not. Nothing surprising about that. George often asked me about "your friend Susan Sontag," wanting to know whether she had come out to us. "Never," I said. "Does she not trust you?" George asked. "That's not it," I said. An answer George never quite believed. Years later, I told him of writers who were close to us and to Susan who occasionally noted that Susan was strangely circumspect when it came to acknowledging that she was gay, or bisexual. Why, these friends asked, did she not speak of it even in interviews where she seemed unable to admit what was obvious? Perhaps just as well, George said. But it was an oddity, wasn't it, that someone as outspoken as Susan should have been reluctant to be publicly identified as gay, even after the AIDS crisis, when remaining in the closet, failing to acknowledge your homosexuality, was considered shameful, dishonest. Though George had no love for Susan, he was astonished when I told him of a dinner we took her to at the Brooklyn home of Larry Nachman, where we talked about Larry's still unfinished work on his Genet essay and about our progress on "the homosexuality issue" we were assembling. At this time, Susan repeated what she'd said before: that if she actually wrote or spoke about her experience of the homosexual scene in New York she'd lose at least half her male friends, who would never forgive her.

7 · CREATIVE DISTORTION

W HEN I think of our many travels with George, his appetite for adventure and conversation, his occasional bad behavior seemed almost to belong to someone else. Of course I'd had my own moments with George when he'd been rude or cutting to someone who deserved better. As I was writing this memoir I received an email from my friend Rosanna Warren who agreed that George was decidedly a worthy subject and that his books mattered, and continue to matter. "And after all," she said, "many of our writer-heroes are hardly 'nice' people." In her few interactions with George, he'd been notably "snotty," she reported, even competitive, and had spoken ungenerously to her about her father, Robert Penn Warren, and her teacher, William Arrowsmith. That George could be abrasive was not in doubt, though it was not the face he most often exhibited. Unbidden, he wrote letters of encouragement to many young poets whose first books he happened to read. Often, he contributed generous comments for the dust jackets of writers and scholars he'd never met.

George's reputation for being other than a "nice man" colored his relations with many who might otherwise have found in him a thrilling and genial presence. That reputation clearly affected the way his books were read by some who couldn't get past what they'd heard of him or witnessed. He knew that Susan Sontag inspired exactly that sort of distaste in people who held against her a particularly callous thing she'd written or said, her resort now and then to a species of bristling condescension. Not surprising that George repeated, more than once, a story I told him about my experience as one of three judges for a nonfiction prize sponsored by the American PEN organization, in a year when far and away the best entry was a posthumous volume, *Arguably*, by Christopher Hitchens. My fellow judges grudgingly conceded that Hitchens could be an unusually arresting prose stylist and a scintillating polemicist, but they found it impossible to offer the prize to someone whose writing seemed to them politically distasteful, some of the time positively indecent.

George thought this anecdote especially telling, and though he never compared himself with Hitchens, they were both erudite polymaths who frequently got under people's skin. When I told George that my fellow judges had come around to Hitchens, after they proposed that I assign to them what I took to be the best ten essays from *Arguably*, he noted that such a turnabout was exceedingly rare, and I wondered if such a reversal might some day be possible for those who had heard too much about the "bad" George.

Some of the attacks George inspired were a matter of honest disagreement. In "Silence and the Poet," did he actually mean that in a culture "which is, increasingly, a wind-tunnel of gossip" and triviality, when "the words in the city are full of savagery and lies, nothing speaks louder than the unwritten poem"?[73] Did he really mean "tactless" when he stressed the signal importance of being tactless and undiplomatic in our efforts to "stay honest with ourselves and our students"? Did he unduly exaggerate, in "Night Words," the dangers entailed

in the widespread availability of pornography, the "total freedom of the uncensored erotic imagination"? Was there, in his
warnings about the new pornographers, who "take away the
words that were of the night and shout them over the rooftops,
making them hollow," too much emphasis on "the new servi-
tude" to a charged and explicit erotic vocabulary that left
"language poorer, less endowed with capacity for fresh
discrimination"?[74] How to assess his suggestion in "A Kind of
Survivor," that as a Jew, he had placed on his own children's
backs "a burden of ancient loathing and set savagery at their
heels. Perhaps we Jews walk closer to our children than other
men; try as they may, they cannot leap out of our shadow"?[75]

These and numerous other observations, however stirring
and refreshing, were also vulnerable to dispute, and there were
those poised to challenge them. "It is Steiner's habit," wrote
Terrence Des Pres, "to push to, and then beyond, frontiers of
established scholarship. Outrageous speculation is, for him,
standard practice, often with splendid results." For Des Pres
and other critics, there was "no doubt about his brilliance," nor
about the importance of his thought on several fronts, whatever the "extravagance" of the theories that Steiner sometimes
pressed. His habit was to make "large claims, most of which he
roots in research as well as intuition"—so Des Pres argued—
and yet one felt now and then that his thesis "cannot be proved,"
whatever its benefits in opening debate in arenas no one else
dared to enter.[76]

A telling moment in George's lengthy *Paris Review* interview in 1995 occurs when he is asked about the reception, and
staying power, of *After Babel*. In responding to such a question
about what may well be his most ambitious and well-received
book, only George would have cited a particular negative
review of his work. The reviewer, whom he describes as "the

high priest of the mandarins," had written that *"After Babel* is a very bad book, but alas it is a classic." George had thanked the reviewer for that assessment, and most especially for his use of the word "alas." But then, George went on, "he wrote me something very interesting. He said we have reached a point where no man can cover the whole field of the linguistics and poetics of translation. This book, he said, should have been written under your guidance by six or seven specialists. So I wrote back, 'No, it should not. It would then be wasted, and end up gathering dust on the technical shelves.' I prefer the enormous risks. There were indeed errors, there were inaccuracies, because a book that's worth living with is the act of one voice, the act of a passion, the act of a *persona*."[77]

Yes, George took risks, and most often proved that they were worth taking, and often earned the opposition he aroused. He took on major thinkers at the height of their influence, targeting missteps, oversights, or omissions in the work of Noam Chomsky, Foucault, and Jacques Derrida. He made the case for writers like Louis-Ferdinand Céline, whose antisemitism and misanthropy were anathema to him, and for others like W. G. Sebald and Thomas Bernhard, who might well have remained obscure without his interventions. Drawn to the singularity of Simone Weil's philosophic rigor and her obsession with "the mystery of God's love," he made a powerful case for her as "a transcendent schlemiel."[78] Although George had written a path-breaking essay on the impact of Nazi propaganda on the German language, he was entirely prepared to celebrate Gunter Grass's achievement when his Danzig trilogy appeared, and he took that occasion as an opportunity to revise and refine what he had earlier proposed about the relationship between political discourse and its disastrous effect on literary language.

Impossible to do more than suggest the force and precision

of George's robust interventions, their transparency of feeling and devastating candor.

On Celine: [M]uch remains puzzling in the cry for massacre which rings through [Celine's work]. . . . Adjuring Western civilization to eliminate all Jews—men, women, and children—and to eradicate their very shadow from mankind, Louis-Ferdinand Celine in these voluminous tracts exhibited virtuosities of detestation, of incitement for which there are, fortunately, few analogues. . . . As one forces oneself to leaf through this or that passage, the flashes of stylistic genius, of verbal incandescence strike one as might a brusque shiver of light across the sheen of a cesspool. (Coleridge noted the transient sparkle of starlight in his brimming chamber pot.)

On Bernhard: Yet even where Thomas Bernhard is less than himself the style is unmistakable. Heir to the marmoreal purity of Kleist's narrative prose and to the vibrancy of terror and surrealism in Kafka, Bernhard has made of the short sentence, of an impersonal, seemingly officious syntax, and of the stripping of individual words to their radical bones an instrument wholly fitted to its excoriating purpose. . . . The black woods, the rushing but often polluted torrents, the sodden, malignant hamlets of Carinthia—the secretive region of Austria in which Bernhard leads his wholly private life—were transmuted into the locale of a small-time inferno. Here human ignorance, archaic detestations, sexual brutality, and social pretense flourish like adders. . . . [But] the trouble with hatred is its shortness of breath. Where hatred generates truly classic inspiration—in Dante, in Swift, in Rimbaud—it does so in spurts, over short distances. Prolonged, it becomes a monotone, a blunted saw buzzing and scraping interminably.

On Weil: By a twist of logic, this young Jew of the French para-Marxist left came to make a series of approbatory comments on Hitler. She lauded his Roman grandeur, his spiritual and administrative seizure of collective hopes and needs. . . . To Weil anything was preferable to the unctuous hypocrisies, corruptions, and facile materialism of bourgeois capitalist democracy. Her ferocities on this issue derive from the burning radicalism of Amos and from Jesus' damning of wealth. They come out of Sparta and Lenin. . . . Like other absolutists of thought, Simon Weil was drawn to violence. Though wrong-headed—she completely misses the festive glitter of archaic heroism—her essay on the *Iliad* does put in high relief the brutalities, the blood lust in the epic. At times, Weil was a pacifist, at other times eager for battle. . . . The eventuality of torture fixed her mind darkly. She sought to rehearse for it. . . . Like Pascal, like certain great painters and narrators of agony (both suffered and inflicted), she imagined materially, she reflected and analyzed with her nerve ends. The politics in her late essays and in her design for France reborn are a fearful but poignant muddle.

On Brecht: Brecht's detestation of bourgeois capitalism remained visceral, his intimations of its impending doom as cheerily anarchic as ever. But much in this prophetic loathing . . . harks back to the bohemian nose-thumbing of his youth and to a kind of Lutheran moralism. His acute antennae told him of the stench of bureaucracy, of the grey petit-bourgeois coercions that prevailed in Mother Russia. Even as Martin Heidegger was during this same time developing an inward, "private National Socialism" (the expression comes from an S.S. file), so Brecht was expounding for and to himself a satiric, analytic Communism alien to Stalinist orthodoxy and also to the simplistic needs of the proletariat and the left intelligentsia in the West.[79]

James Wood, despite his attack on Steiner's works in the *New Republic*, noted that he was always "much more open to new work, in various languages, than is usual among English-language critics," and he recalled that "there are people who speak happily of their years at Cambridge University in the sixties, when the young Steiner filled lecture rooms, burrowing into his cellular erudition, prompting students to discover writers who were hardly known to them: Borges, Barthes, Garcia Márquez, Beckett. . . . Now most of them are available in English, and Steiner had something to do with this."[80]

Had I read the new Margaret Atwood novel, George asked unexpectedly at our dinner table one night, or Geoffrey Hill's new poems, and then went on talking about those writers as if he had just read them that morning. "You must read the *Malina* novel by Ingeborg Bachmann," George suddenly said one day at a London bookstore. "I imagine you know only her poems, but the novel will be life-changing." So much so that I was soon teaching *Malina* in my classes and publishing essays on Bachmann in *Harper's* and elsewhere. Like legions of readers, I often found myself following George's leads.

Once at a public lecture in Boston, when George was cited

as a critic who "perpetuates female marginality," I raised my hand to enquire what exactly the lecturer meant. She replied that George had described aesthetic creativity as "an act of God 'himself.'" Emphasis on "himself." Was that it? I asked. There's more, I was assured, though no further details were forthcoming. Not then. Had I been a panelist, I'd have helped out the speaker by citing a few other provocative speculations, of the sort that Steiner was in the habit of occasionally dropping. But then I'd have gone on to note that he was more than ready to promote women writers, not only Atwood and Bachmann, but Doris Lessing, Anne Carson, Gertrude Schnackenberg, A. S. Byatt, and Edna O'Brien. In an issue of the *Times Literary Supplement*, when several writers were asked to select a "Best Book of the Year," George recommended the work of a writer whose work was reissued by Virago after forty years:

> Sylvia Townsend Warner's *The Corner That Held Them* strikes one as a masterpiece. As an act of imagined history—the life of a fenland nunnery in the fourteenth century—this novel has few rivals. Warner conveys the strange ordinariness of a distant yet immediate past with utter authority. But her chronicle of lives under pressure, at once visionary and petty, makes for a fiction of extreme density. No one after Hardy has interwoven more closely the sheer feel of material things, of weather, of light across water or foliage, with the inward landscapes of character. The prose precisely matches the theme and settings: it is at once bone-spare and of a rich and troubling opacity. A classic, whose resonance deepens inside the reader in proportion to its austere, luminous discretion. Also, as it happens, a work of high, frequent comedy.[81]

Steiner was unquestionably a major force for enlightenment. In bookstores in France, Italy, Germany, and Spain, the dust jackets of novels and biographies, scholarly and philosophical works carried comments from his reviews and blurbs. International symposia at universities in several European countries were convened to debate his theories about language, the Holocaust, the death of tragedy, and other controversial topics, where he was always willing to present himself as a target for other participants who wished to challenge him.

George was a superb reader and an inspired teacher. Terence Des Pres was hardly alone in noting that Steiner "amply demonstrates the centrality of what might be called 'productive error' or 'creative distortion'" in his close readings. In a book like *Antigones*, Des Pres wrote, "Steiner not only uncovers splendid moments of 'creative distortion' in the works of others, but employs it himself."[82] More than once over the years I asked George whether by "creative distortion" he meant what he called "a going against the grain of what seems indisputable in a text, even a canonical work"?

"Look," he said, "what sounds to you like a wild assertion really captures what is done more often than you think. Consider what happens when a translator does what needs to be done to transmit a masterwork in another language. You can see this for yourself, Robert, when you place alongside one another two competing versions of an original and ask yourself why one is so much superior to the other."

Actually, I had attempted to make such comparisons frequently, not grasping what made for the decisive difference. Was it not merely local, semantic? Was it not the case that often a given translation was superior to another simply because one translator was a better writer? But more than that was involved, George argued, in comparing a Robert Lowell "imitation" of a

Montale poem with a more "correct" or standard translation of the same poem: It wasn't just that Lowell was, as a poet, vastly superior to even a competent translator, but he was more adept at "creative distortion." Wasn't that so? That Lowell took what some would call unforgivable liberties in altering an original?

Des Pres, clearly wanting to grasp better than I had the nature of such "creative distortion," wrote in his review of George's *Antigones* about passages where George "celebrates Hölderlin's eccentric translation of *Antigone*, which is the greater for its manifest mistakes." Emphatic words: "the greater for its manifest mistakes." Des Pres explains that for Steiner, "There is the Greek text by Sophocles, lucid but unrealized; then there is the 'Hesperian' text created by the translator, in this case Hölderlin, who liberates and brings to fulfillment the sacred meaning sealed in the original. Hölderlin's mad translation thus becomes an act of 'reading against' the Greek, an accomplishment truer to Sophocles than Sophocles himself was able to be."[83]

When I spoke with George about Des Pres's review—it appeared immediately after the notorious Edward Said essay in the same issue of the *Nation* magazine (1985)—he cited what we'd both once heard from the poet-translator Ben Belitt, that Borges much preferred the English translations of his poems to their Spanish language originals, feeling that the English versions captured something that his own language could not express. I don't doubt that an aspect of "creative distortion" figured in those translations by audacious poets like Belitt (who himself was on the receiving end of much criticism about his translations).

Still, the very notion of creative distortion continued to trouble me, and whenever I raised the issue, George would say that I was mistaken to think of it as a violation, an offense against an original undertaken by someone too careless or cavalier to register the sin. Think, George would suggest, of what actually occurs when you're making a translation—as you do, must do, every time you hear something and process it. All "interpretative reception," George insisted, is translation. Even when we receive messages in nonverbal situations we must engage in translation. You do understand, George explained, that we never mean exactly what we say, and that we may never hope to penetrate confidently to the substance of another person's words or signs. Is it not clear that our own utterances intentionally or unconsciously mask half of what we feel, so that we translate our sentiments into a shorthand of plausible and frequently inoffensive commonplaces?

These propositions—my words, George's ideas—were at the heart of *After Babel*, and they were entirely of a piece with his other books and essays in which his intent was to read everything with a disciplined alertness to distortion. In some respects the most liberating aspect of this stance was his insistence on combat, a dialectic of constraint and aggression, of "interanimation." That is what happens, he argued, when we attempt to appropriate to our own perspective the utterances, or meanings, or signals inscribed in an adverse text or communication issuing from someone not ourselves. We want to acknowledge in each transaction, he argued, the "almost bewildering bias of the human spirit towards freedom." We want also to honor the otherness of the alien text or message and to operate with the sense that, whatever our inclination to creative distortion, there are constraints we must be willing to observe.

When we discussed similar matters, he would often laugh mischievously. And when I told him that he had made perfectly clear what others had been unable to explain with comparable lucidity, he would note there were gaps in his own understanding of the relevant factors. Gaps he sought to fill, without complete success. Is there reason, George would ask, to think that we appreciate this particular line in Sophocles only when we set it alongside this particular line in Shakespeare? Does music inspired by Sophocles—compositions by Carl Orff or Honegger—open up the original in a drastic and indispensable way? When we study the speech patterns of lovers in a wide range of works over centuries, do we not observe that masculine "intonations dull after orgasm," indicating something essential about the language peculiar to males? And is it not true that, in the utterances of women characters, there is a radically divergent "speech mythology," wherein men will often seem erotic liars and "incorrigible" braggarts, worthy of being mocked, the male a creature "who uses language to cover up his sexual or professional fiascos, his infantile needs."

George's willingness to travel to such places invariably yielded uncommon insights, and considerable, if intermittent, opposition. For George, the creative distortion entailed in diverging from the dull, steady pursuit of stationary targets was not only exhilarating but essential, and it made of his own criticism at its best a dramatically compelling and imaginative achievement.

8 · "I WISH YOU HADN'T DONE THAT"

A GOOD many literary people, even those much drawn to theory, suppose that there is a yawning gap between those who elaborate ambitious ideas and others more disposed to infer what they can from a close reading of a text. Our leading literary critic, James Wood, has never endorsed the notion of such a gap, but in his critiques of Steiner's work he does argue that Steiner is too given to "imprecisions and melodramas," and he cites Vladimir Nabokov, who "complained that one of Steiner's essays was 'built on solid abstractions and opaque generalizations.'"[84] George was fully alert to such complaints. When he submitted an essay for *Salmagundi* I would occasionally recommend that he look more closely at one of the texts to which he had glancingly alluded on the way to the next stage in his argument. Rarely did he take me up on such recommendations, and on a few occasions we talked about what would be lost, or gained, by doing what I proposed. In effect, George would say, you are asking me for something I am prepared to do in another sort of piece, whereas this one was conceived as a lecture, not a close reading. Fair enough, I often felt, and although there are occasional "melodramas" in George's work, they never seemed to me disabling.

Isaiah Berlin had complained of Steiner's melodramas in a Reader's Report for Oxford University Press, responding to the manuscript of *Antigones*. "Tantalizing," wrote Berlin, "irritating, exciting, maddening . . ." "Too much the tendency," Berlin wrote, "to put all his goods . . . in the shop window," too much "uncontrolled" mention of not always strictly relevant though often "arresting paradoxes." To which Henry Hardy, the editor of Berlin's papers as well as the author of an important book on Berlin,[85] suggested in a letter to the editor of the *Times Literary Supplement*, "Similar criticism might be leveled at Berlin himself—not unrhapsodic, nor the most scrupulous of scholars—and there may be a tinge of self-criticism in his attitude to his fellow Jew."[86]

As for "opaque generalizations," the best I can say is "I think not." Nabokov was rarely a reliable judge of literary or linguistic theory or of individual writers. One has only to read his lectures on Dostoyevsky and his haughty dismissals of Solzhenitsyn and other major writers to see his notorious shortcomings. Steiner could not have taken too much to heart the criticism of a man who described both T. S. Eliot and Thomas Mann as "such big fakes," and *Crime and Punishment* as "incredibly banal."

But he did surely take note of "George Steiner's Unreal Presence," a review by James Wood published in the *New Republic*,[87] where the author was an associate literary editor, and where I was a frequent contributor. Wood seemed to me one of the most intelligent younger critics in the English-speaking world. His essay troubled me because he had a gift for spotting lapses or characteristic weaknesses in the more sweepingly audacious—occasionally wrong-headed—of George's essays, while refusing to concede that in a great many books and essays George had done things for which Wood, like the rest of us, must surely have been grateful. I felt that, in a summing up, writers should be assessed principally in terms of their best work. In my view, Wood's essay read like a summing up, and so I wondered why he would not credit what was obvious—for example what Alfred Kazin had noted, that "Steiner transmits the world of European literature and thought to American audiences better than anyone now writing."[88]

Steiner was sometimes "vague," Wood argued, when he ought to have been most rigorous, as in proposing a thesis ("real presences") Wood found impossible to support. He hated Steiner's tendency to suppose that when works made him feel "somewhat religious," the works themselves were in fact "somewhat religious." He hated what he called "the leap into sublimity," Steiner's inclination to raise "goose bumps" when confronted by art and ideas he admired.

Even for me, Wood's essay was a literary performance of considerable virtuosity and insight, an essay that George himself would have much admired had it been directed at some other writer about whom he shared the operant sentiments. The sentences bristle and burn with a polemic urgency, and Wood is especially impressive in demanding of Steiner a "theological accountability" that he nowhere finds in George's references to "the quasi-divine." Wood finds laughable the following passage, in which Steiner acknowledges his inability to process what seems to him astonishing: "The picture of some man or woman, lunching, dining, after he or she had 'invented' and set down these and certain other biblical texts, leaves me, as it were, blinded and off balance." Wood's conclusion, that "in the end all [Steiner] offers is a hedged secularism written up religiously," is a fitting close to the argument he has strenuously marshalled, though it does also lead me to wonder why Steiner's frank acknowledgment of goose bumps and blindness should have provoked in Wood only derision. When Steiner says it "defies my grasp" that Kafka's parable "Before the Law" can have been written by a man "going to and from his daily insurance," Wood replies, "And indeed it does," and then declares, "Truly, this is not thought, but a fear of thought."

Do the words "defies my grasp" signify "a fear of thought"? Those words—"a fear of thought"—hardly describe Steiner. Did readers of the *New Yorker* find a fear of thought in Steiner's rigorous interrogations of Noam Chomsky, Gershom Scholem, Simone Weil, or Claude Levi-Strauss? Did Steiner's densely argued, unfailingly lucid book on Heidegger—which Wood casually refers to as "very good"—betray "a fear of thought"? It is hard not to feel that the arguments Wood assembles rely upon a highly selective attention to a few passages in essays chosen precisely for their apparent vulnerability to the charge Wood wished to make. Wood sharply disparages what he calls Steiner's "rather dramatic binarisms," his tendency to be astonished that a Nazi official could cultivate "a knowledge of Goethe [or] a love of Rilke," that a traitor in the employ of Soviet intelligence, like the art historian Anthony Blunt, could regard "a false attribution of a Watteau drawing [as] a sin against the spirit." But these "binarisms" hardly seem incidental to the case Steiner makes, and he is frank about the degree to which his own generative insights are rooted in hypotheses open to dispute.

That frankness is everywhere apparent in Steiner's work, even in a highly demanding, densely argued philosophical work like *Real Presences*.[89] There Steiner insistently probes the mysteries of reception, the unanswerable questions that we are apt to ask about our susceptibility to works of art. Wood found Steiner's "religiose language" fatally misleading, and scrupulously explained why, and though I was not fully persuaded, I did have my own questions about a book that never seemed to me fully satisfactory. In fact, when it first appeared, I commissioned three critics to elucidate the thorny issues opened up by *Real Presences* for a 1990 issue of *Salmagundi*. Those formidable critics did not find Steiner's refusal to "play it cool"—in what he calls "bearing witness to the poetic"—at all lame or disabling. They were moved by Steiner's willingness "to risk the whole gamut of muddle and embarrassment" in an effort to "tell of what happens inside oneself as one affords vital welcome and habitation" to works of art that take hold of us.

Throughout *Real Presences*—so I have always believed—Steiner conveys the sense that he is earnestly working to understand things that do somewhat exceed his full understanding. That Wood was not moved by any of this seemed to me surprising, and in thinking again about the gap between his take on the book and mine, I am drawn to a passage like the following from Steiner:

> Cheap music, childish images, the vulgate in language, in its crassest sense, can penetrate to the deeps of our necessities and dreams. . . . The opening bars, the hammer-beat accelerando of Edith Piaf's "Je ne regrette rien"—the text is infantile, the tune stentorious, and the politics which enlisted the song unattractive—tempt every nerve in me, touch the bone with a cold burn and draw me after into God knows what infidelities to reason, each time I hear the song, and hear it, uncalled for, recurrent inside me. Wagner raged at his inability to excise from within his remembrance and involuntary humming, the tin-pot tunes of a contemporary operetta. . . .There are rhymes, puns, jingle effects flat as stale water, which mesmerize not only

readers and listeners but the greatest of poets (Will Shakespeare on will; Victor Hugo in hundredfold thrall to ombre / sombre). . . . It is as if the honeycomb of each individual receptivity, of each individual psychic indwelling, were intricately specific.

And where does such reflection lead us? In many directions, to be sure, but one in particular is central to the picture Steiner composes. Each of us will have our own way of describing and attempting to penetrate what happens to us when a song or painting or poem takes hold of us. "Each account," Steiner writes, "each attempt at paraphrase or metaphoric approximation will prove inadequate in its own way. There is, in essence, common ground. But no individual telling of the possession by and possession of felt form and meaning quite translates into any other."

Wood contends that, in making such concessions and identifying what seems to him mysterious, Steiner merely "affects the motions of argument" while actually "standing completely still." This seemed to me quite misleading as regards *Real Presences*, but a shrewd assessment in the case of a single piece called "Archives of Eden"—a speech George had written as the keynote lecture for a 1980 *Salmagundi* conference on "Art & Intellect in America." There, as Wood argued, Steiner only pretended "to see things from the American side" in his efforts to contrast American democracy with the tyranny, vanity, and corruption that produced—among other things—the high achievements of European culture.

But why, I continued to wonder, did Wood—given his avowed familiarity with "much of Steiner's work"—not acknowledge the obvious: that in his major works, from *Language and Silence*, *Tolstoy or Dostoevsky*, and *The Death of Tragedy* to *After Babel*,

On Difficulty, *Extraterritorial*, and *Antigones*, the motions of argument are fully in the service of a strenuous effort to get to the bottom of ideas and sensations by no means fully settled. Mysterious. George could only think of Wood's antipathy as deeply personal. Though he knew that a book like *Real Presences* was vulnerable to criticism, he wondered at the enormous gap between its mainly negative reception in the United States and its reception elsewhere. "It's being studied in European universities," he wrote me in a letter of January 30, 1992, "is in its sixth French printing, is passing 10,000 in Germany and being bought for translation throughout the eastern countries. . . . Julia Kristeva debates my book with me on BBC-TV this Saturday in London, and Hans Kung is doing a three-day meeting on the book next November in Tubingen." No suggestion here that therefore the book would meet no resistance, but it did clearly seem not to merit the kind of ridicule Wood had heaped upon it.

The least interesting thing to say about Wood's attack on Steiner is that it was ungenerous. No one who writes criticism can afford to be unfailingly generous. Surely Steiner was not always generous, though his colleague John Updike described him as "one of the most generous" of *New Yorker* critics. My own feeling about the Wood review was that it was a stirring, often brilliant, young man's take-down of an older writer, and in truth Wood himself conceded (in a later interview) that his assault was perhaps a bit much. Its tone gave off an air of irritation, as if Wood were responding to an offense. He derided what he called George's "first night flamboyance, as if we were his virgins in knowledge." And so Wood was disposed not to be generous, but to dispense his enmity, as he was to do in many of his early essays, in which the targets he aimed to demolish included a number of the most ambitious and original writers in the country—from Thomas Pynchon and Don DeLillo to Toni Morrison. In each of those essays there was much to learn, much to admire. At his best Wood could be both contentious and exhilarating, as many of us had rightly said of Steiner.

In the end, and again, I objected principally to the character of Wood's piece as a kind of summing up. Though a great many readers of a magazine like the *New Republic* had read George's reviews, and some had surely read one or more of his books, there were others who would perhaps come away from Wood's piece believing that Steiner could be readily dismissed as a writer who had promoted three or four untenable and preposterous notions and miraculously won for himself a credulous readership. This I was not prepared to accept.

What to do in the face of Wood's bravura performance? Nothing, would seem the appropriate answer. Applause perhaps. A sly letter of appreciation containing just a sentence or two of reprimand. The letter directed to the critic himself or to the editor? It occurred to me that George would not wish to contend with such an essay. Nothing to be gained. The argument mounted in the essay too close grained and detailed to be answered in anything less than an essay of comparable scope. And even then maybe there would be little hope of successfully countering several of the main thrusts inspired principally by two Steiner essays—both delivered as public lectures and both highly speculative and aggressively opinionated.

But if George had no desire to enter the lists in this instance, I saw no reason why I should not. Absurd to think that I would presume to speak on his behalf, and yet I did wish to speak for myself and for others who might hope to correct the record. Had Wood framed his essay strictly as a focused response to several particularly vulnerable Steiner essays—like those I had published in the pages of *Salmagundi* magazine—I'd have thought good, fair enough. However, it seemed necessary to assert that George deserved better in an assessment that purported to be a verdict on an entire career and on an enormous body of scholarship and criticism. A reader of Wood's piece who had managed, somehow, to be ignorant of George's work over four decades would be led to think that Steiner was at best an erudite fellow whose penchant for the histrionic and tendentious had led him perpetually astray. That reader would have been astonished to learn that George was a persistently close reader of the works he cited. Often in his books, long passages focused on words, phrases, accents, and idioms at the heart of the arguments he constructed. Perhaps more importantly, Wood's attack on George had failed to acknowledge that George was widely accorded the kind of attention characteristically directed at a thinker who had substantially affected an entire discipline or field of study.

And so I fired off a letter to Leon Wieseltier, literary editor of the *New Republic*, who had so often commissioned my own reviews and essays. I argued that in spite of the many attacks leveled at Steiner there was a more than substantial record of admiration and support from leading writers and intellectuals. That George's books were translated into dozens of languages and included in the curricula of major universities all over the world. Would not a reader of Wood's essay want to have some sense of that part of the record?

It was also important, to ask why, if George was principally the contentious "museum of European monuments" Wood had painted, he had managed to fool so many of the best minds in the world over so many years. I pointed out that the *New Republic* had published favorable reviews of virtually every one of Steiner's books, and that the reviewers included several of the country's most distinguished scholars in each of the relevant scholarly domains. To be sure, George had written, in *Real Presences*, that "the relativity, the arbitrariness of all aesthetic propositions, of all value-judgments is inherent in human consciousness" and that "anything can be said about anything." Judgments about the worth of George's work, even coming from the most distinguished scholars in a range of disciplines, could, as George wrote, "never quite be anything but more or less persuasive."

Could it be that each of those eminent reviewers—philosophers, linguists, Russian scholars, and scholars of German and Jewish culture—were deceived about the scruple and originality of Steiner's scholarship? That Bernard Knox, the director of Hellenic Studies in Washington—to cite but one of those names—did not know what he was talking about when he praised George's *Antigones* for its "incisive analysis," its "challenging" insights, its commitment to close reading ("forcefully demonstrated in his 45-page exegesis" of "140 lines of verse" in Sophocles), and its "compelling" excursions into Kierkegaard, Hegel, and other major thinkers?[90] Citing these formidable reviewers seemed to me the most persuasive feature of my letter, and I fully anticipated its publication, and that James Wood would deploy his more than formidable skills to answer it.

To my dismay, I received a short letter from Wieseltier, indicating that "of course" he would not publish the letter. Would not. "Could not." Which probably should have ended the episode. I then sent the letter to fourteen prominent *New Republic* contributors, asking them to cosign my letter and, when seven agreed to cosign, I re-sent the letter to Wieseltier, who again refused to publish it and "wished you hadn't done that." A signal, I thought, that my long association with the magazine would end with this altercation, for which I had only myself to blame—though very soon I was forgiven, or excused, and went on to publish many more review-essays in the magazine, on writers like John Updike and Philip Roth and less well-known writers like Fleur Jaeggy and Norman Manea.

And what of my relations with James Wood? George never again mentioned the piece to me after an initial reference to it in a letter, not even years later when we rehearsed the many trials to which he had been subjected. Not even when a new issue of *Salmagundi* came out some years later containing a substantial interview with Wood. Not even when I told him of a lecture Wood had delivered at my invitation at Skidmore College, or of my friendship with Wood's wife, Claire Messud, whose works I taught at the college and in my graduate courses at The New School for Social Research in Manhattan.

What I never spoke of with George were the extraordinary letters Wood had sent me immediately following the rejection of my letters to the editor. These were personal letters in which he assured me that he had urged Wieseltier to publish what I had written to defend George. Though Wood made a few concessions, he used these lengthy letters to insist that he stood by what he had written, and underlined the key complaints he had elaborated in his essay. But he also declared that he was touched by my defense of Steiner, and allowed himself to hope that when he began to publish books of his own he would have me, or someone like me, to defend him against what were sure to be comparably harsh criticisms.

Not long after the Steiner episode, Wood accompanied Claire to Saratoga Springs, where she was to teach for a week at my invitation—as she has continued to do for many years— in the New York State Summer Writers Institute. At once it was clear to me that these were people I could do nothing but adore and esteem. That James Wood and I disagreed about

Steiner—also about some of the other writers he had eviscer-
ated—was no bar to a developing friendship, a friendship close
enough that we were able to speak now and again about
George, especially in the years of his old age, when he could
no longer travel, and Peg and I often visited him at his home
in Cambridge.

When I think of the best literary essayists of the past half
century, I think often of George, of Susan, and of James. The
larger case for Steiner must include not only the major essays
but the scholarly and critical books. He was a great reviewer-
critic, but he was also a scholar and a thinker to be reckoned
with. For a long time I felt there was not much to set beside a
dozen Sontag essays and George's essays on Borges and Brecht,
Celine and Beckett, Lukacs and Mann, "Eros and Idiom," chess
and treason.

And then, like many other readers, I found in Wood's essays
a comparable genius and range. The heft and delicacy of his
writing about Woolf and W. G. Sebald, Italo Svevo and Chek-
hov, D. H. Lawrence and Saul Bellow, Joseph Roth and V. S.
Naipaul's *Mister Biswas*, have made his work as indispensable to
me as Steiner's best writing.

My secret wish, when I edited *George Steiner at the New Yorker*
for New Directions in 2009—at the time when Wood had suc-
ceeded Steiner as a senior book critic for the *New Yorker*—was
that James would review the book and declare that George
Steiner was every bit as good as I thought he was. That he
would say my selection of George's *New Yorker* pieces was
inspired (!!!), and note what an earlier critic, Naomi Bliven,
wrote about him in the *New Yorker*: "He is frequently ironic and
witty, but for the most part his language and his ideas display
even handedness, seriousness without heaviness, learning
without pedantry, and sober charm."[91] That Wood would go

on to say of Steiner what I always feel when I read a new essay by Wood himself: that one of the principal reasons for reading him is the sheer pleasure of his prose—along with the other virtues cited in reviews of George's work: "subtlety and acuteness," to be sure, and also the willingness to go forward "slap in the teeth of the prevailing wind."

9 · AN ACADEMY OF ONE

WHEN George died in February of 2020 at the age of ninety, the obituary notices in the European press were astonishingly laudatory. In *Le Monde, Le Figaro, La Repubblica, Die Zeit*, the *Guardian, El Pais*, and *Nazione*, George, a self-described "mere critic" and "courier," was memorialized as a "polymath devoted to the ideal of literacy."[92] Some American papers carried fulsome expressions of remembrance; George's son, David, emailed me Adam Gopnik's *New Yorker* tribute, writing that this was the memorial George would have most appreciated. Several sentences are worth citing, but those that correct common misperceptions are essential, including the oft-repeated slur that Steiner was "pretentious." Gopnik writes: "'Pretentious,' though a word journalists sometimes used to describe [Steiner], was the last thing he ever was. He was never pretending. He was a humanities faculty in himself, an academy of one."[93]

And Gopnik amends another erroneous misperception by noting that Steiner's brand of seriousness was "genuine, and not merely patrician."

George often worried that, for all of his ambition and achievement, he had failed. He was sensitive even to the verdicts handed down by critics whose assessment should not have bothered him at all. In a letter of January 1985 agreeing to deliver a dinner talk on "'An Unenlightened View of History' to ten or twelve invited guests at your home," he alludes to a "short piece by [Robert] Alter saying I have failed in my best to be of the truly great, to be 'a Freud or a Marx,' and have therefore also missed 'the second rank—such as Derrida or Leavis.' . . . It has all been in vain, he rules, 'and it is now too late for Steiner.' He may or may not be right. He probably is. What has interested me is the kind of reactions elicited in one's psyche and body as one reads and re-reads such a death sentence."

George was in his mid-fifties when he wrote that letter, and continued writing books and essays for another thirty years. No doubt few of us who entertain one degree or another of high ambition ever think "to be of the truly great," and few writers and thinkers dare to compare themselves even to the so-called "second rank" figures who exert enormous influence on their contemporaries and are then soon forgotten. Often I did what I could to persuade George that it was a mistake to dwell on his achievement in such terms, and he knew that I thought his best work magnificent and apt to be enduring.

Over the years, when I got worked up about this or that slur George was subjected to, I reminded myself that derision and contempt were by no means unusual for writers who had made a difference by traveling to places others feared to enter. George didn't write to win approval. He was often in opposition to the established consensus. That was his way of opening a path to the heart of the issues and ambivalences he wished to understand. "There are in all periods," Christopher Hitchens wrote, "people who feel themselves in some fashion to be apart. . . . [To be in opposition] is something you are and not something you do."[94] George was a loyal and passionate friend, and yet in significant ways he was always apart. Apart as Hannah Arendt was often apart, or V. S. Naipaul, or Hitchens. Though I was not fortunate enough to be a friend of Hannah Arendt, I was her student during the period in the early 1960s when she was often characterized as a self-hating anti-Semite, and her book *Eichmann in Jerusalem* was attacked as foul and offensive by Gershom Scholem and other leading scholars.

In fact, when I asked Sir Isaiah Berlin in 1978 to contribute an essay on Hannah Arendt to a special issue of *Salmagundi* devoted to her work, he wrote—as a *Salmagundi* contributor who clearly admired the magazine—to express his amazement at the notion that Arendt could conceivably be a "worthy subject." What could I possibly be thinking, Berlin asked. George had good company in the ranks of those who stirred ferocious antagonism, and he would not have been surprised to learn that Levi-Strauss, a thinker whose work he had championed, has at last inspired a host of furious detractors, not merely because his work no longer seems to them adequately scientific, but because his views on decolonization and tradition no longer seem to accord with notions fashionable in Western academic circles.

In the summer of 2019, Peg and I visited the Steiners in Cambridge and sat with them for nearly two hours upstairs in their bedroom, where they were attended by a live-in nurse. George was animated, apologizing for his recumbent posture, but eager for news. What was our violinist son Gabe playing these days? Who had written the blurbs for my new book? He was tired, he said, was always tired. Zara took the lead and asked me to recount my initial meetings with George, which I did, describing him as the ball-buster he could sometimes be. Which made all of us laugh, and provoked Zara to say, "Yes, that's George, you've got him."

George remembered that a year earlier I had sent him "a last letter," at the urging of his son, David, who didn't believe that his parents would last to our next scheduled visit. By then George was no longer writing letters, and each month, when I sent off one of my own, I knew there would be no reply. In that last letter I urged him to read a poem I had enclosed by my friend Robert Pinsky, an elegy called "Impossible to Tell," in which two very good Jewish jokes were embedded. "I tried," said George, "to remember the jokes in that poem you sent, and yet I can't seem to do it."

"No matter. Not now."

"But I do remember what you wrote to me about Philip Roth. That when he died in 2018, there were the tributes but also the tide of disparagement."

"Not surprising, really, do you think?" I asked. The disparagement directed at Roth built mainly on the notion that Roth had had his chance and that now it was time for others with a healthier view of men and women and sex and life to have their turn. A healthier view. That was about it. "Some of it very nasty," I said, "like the voices of people who enjoy dancing on the graves of the recently dead."

"Roth would have known what to do with that," said George. "He would have known. What was it I used to quote from Karl Kraus? Something about the man who gladly does without the praise of the crowd."

"Not his best aphorism," I said.

"You'll have to help me," said George. "Finish the aphorism or tell me a better one."

"I'll give you Kraus's best one," I said. "Or one of the best. How about, 'My language is the common prostitute that I turn into a virgin'"?[95]

"You won't do better than that," George said.

At which point the housekeeper entered the room with two trays of dinner. Peg and I got up to leave, and heard George say as we reached the door, "You know, of course, that this is the last time we shall ever see one another." To which Peg replied, "You've said that before."

"But, my dear," George said, "this time is different."

THREE

AFTERWORD

I s it "awkward" to praise your friends? To defend them? More awkward, perhaps, to criticize them? An interviewer for a European newspaper, to whom I'd spoken of this work in progress on Sontag and Steiner in the spring of 2021, asked these questions and was surprised when I told him I had no misgivings. My two "impossible" friends would not have been shocked by anything I had to say about them. Embarrassed maybe, by certain revealing vignettes, though not for long. They knew I admired and often celebrated them. They also knew that we disagreed about several matters and that I worried about their susceptibility to bad behavior. They would have known that in memoir there is an instinct to candor, and that "too much information" is a besetting temptation even for someone as "nice" as they both took me to be.

Now and then I find it necessary to remind myself that not everyone is apt to care as much as I do about George Steiner and Susan Sontag. Most of those who read Benjamin Moser's biography of Sontag will not likely have gone on to read her books or to teach them. A fair number of those readers have emailed me questions about her sexual partners and her political affiliations, but when I ask younger colleagues if they've read *On Photography* or *Under the Sign of Saturn*, they say no. Susan worried late in life that she might seem important principally for the causes she championed and the glamorous people she knew, rather than for her books. Would she have been pleased or amused by the Sontag dolls sold at the Metropolitan Museum of Art's *Camp/Notes on Fashion* exhibition in 2018? I expect not. And though it never occurred to George that he would be remembered mainly for any causes he championed or the company he kept, he did entertain the thought that he would count mainly as what one critic called "the polymath's polymath," the supreme autodidact, a phenomenon rather than a great writer or thinker.[96]

George had much to say about "criticism" and critics. Like Sontag he viewed criticism—political, literary, cultural—as a secondary pursuit, and critics mainly as "outriders, hangers-on, or shadows to lions." Not the real thing. "The great mass of criticism," he wrote—at a time when he was just beginning to establish himself as one of the leading critics in the world—"is ephemeral, bordering on journalism or straightforward literary history, on a spurt of personal impression scarcely sustained, or on the drab caution of traditional erudite assent."[97] George came of age when poets and fiction writers thought they were living in an "age of criticism," and it did not escape his notice that Sontag rose to fame and celebrity not as the author of novels or films, but as a critic. And yet, he insisted, "very few critics survive in their own right,"[98] and in the main, those we most remember are great poets like T. S. Eliot. Now and then I proposed that he think of criticism not simply as the close reading of texts, or the passing of judgments, or the correction of derelictions of taste.

"Of course," he would say. "Obviously it's more than that, or can be."

"But then why," I would ask, "the insistence on the secondariness of the entire enterprise? Why not think of yourself as an essayist and provocateur who is a thinker, a scholar, and also—dreaded word—a mere 'critic' or 'courier' bringing the news about what is worthy and what is dreck? Why not accept that at your best people like you and Sontag are committed to disturbing the peace of your contemporaries and disturbing the complacencies to which most of us are inured?"

Like George, Susan devoted a good deal of attention to critics and criticism. She not only revered writer-critics and essayists like Roland Barthes, Elias Canetti, and Walter Benjamin, but asked herself why she took such writers as her "masters." These writers were not in any usual sense "critics," though they wrote critical essays and might well have wondered why they, too, were consigned to secondariness. But then they enjoyed their in-between status, and did not think of themselves as mere reporters or dispensers of information. They were not propagandists or censors. Like Steiner and Sontag, these masters were adept at generating "ideas about anything," as Susan liked to say, and whatever their occasional inclination to polemic, "the deepest impulse of [their] temperament" had principally to do with "sharing [their] passions." Their instinct as writers was to be always interesting and to spur themselves and their readers to take on "freedoms and risks." Both shared with Canetti a "fear of not being insolent or ambitious enough." [99] Both were envied and resented for their brashness and even for the breadth of their reading, and their confidence could seem an affront to those who thought it pretentious or unbecoming.

"There is a terrible, mean American resentment," Susan wrote, "toward a writer who tries to do many things," who dares to tackle subjects "guarded by academic and professional dragons." [100] What astonished her, she said, was the "ingratitude" this resentment entailed, ingratitude for the species of brilliance or just sheer critical intelligence exhibited by a writer who was singular and exemplary. Such "mean American resentment" was inspired by Susan's unwillingness to invest in petty doctrinal quarrels, and by George's erudition and eloquence. Both disappointed otherwise enthusiastic readers by resisting the notion that compelling ideas or artworks were required to be socially useful or uplifting.

I WAS MOVED to write this memoir when I learned of George's death. I wanted, of course, to bring him to life as I knew him. But I also wanted to make a case for him and his work, to argue that he did many things we have need of still, that there is something indispensable in the species of intransigence he embodied. There was in him what Sontag once called "a willingness to serve" and also a will to be "magnificent" in the way his work was often said to be. As I proceeded to write, I thought more and more that Susan, too, was essential to this project. Much though she wanted not to be associated with George, she would surely have understood that together they represented a version of "criticism" that is now exceedingly rare. Why so? In part because the academy in this country, and much of the serious media culture, has become a kind of surveillance culture in which the free exercise of critical intelligence can seem suspicious, dangerous, even punishable. But then also because the leisurely, demanding, chastening critical essay we associate with Sontag and Steiner is a form most readers find eminently resistible in an age of the internet where the quick fix is as much as we can handle.

But let me not close with a sour assessment of where we stand. Better, by far, to propose that we commit ourselves again to the species of essayistic writing that is dramatic, unsystematic, eloquent, erudite, and marked, above all, by what Sontag called "the mind's earnest play." That is what principally turned on my two brilliant friends—exemplars, both of them, of what

Sontag celebrated as "intellectual insatiability," both committed to the idea of the writer as the "age's noble adversary,"
poised to defend "tension, exertion, moral and amoral seriousness." That George and Susan were also improbable adepts of
friendship is perhaps the least persuasive thing I can say about
them. Contrary, polarizing, sometimes abrasive, both could
seem at times unlovable. And yet how not to love them for the
life force and intellectual exhilaration they embodied?

NOTES

[1] Ralph Waldo Emerson, *The Conduct of* Life (Boston, MA: Ticknor and Fields, 1860).

[2] John Carroll, "George Steiner and Cambridge English: A Dismal Case of Rancor," *Meanjin Quarterly* (Melbourne: Melbourne University Publishing), September 1, 1973.

[3] Quoted in Robert Boyers, "George Steiner as Cultural Critic: Confronting America," *New England Review* 15, no. 2 (1993).

[4] George Steiner, *Language and Silence: Essays on Language, Literature, and the Inhuman* (New York: Atheneum, 1986).

[5] Susan Sontag, "Speaking Itself," speech at Town Hall in New York City; reprinted in "Communism and the Left," *Nation*, February 27, 1982.

[6] Philip Green, "Comments," *Nation*, February 27, 1982.

[7] Daniel Singer, "Comments," *Nation*, February 27, 1982.

[8] David Hollinger, "Comments," *Nation*, February 27, 1982.

[9] Christopher Hitchens, "Comments," *Nation*, February 27, 1982.

[10] Jenni Diski, "Cuddlesome: Germaine Greer," *London Review of Books* 26, no. 1 (January 2004).

[11] Elias Canetti, speech delivered in Vienna to honour Hermann Broch's fiftieth birthday, November 1936, quoted in Susan Sontag, "Mind as Passion," *Under the Sign of Saturn* (New York: Farrar, Straus and Giroux, 1980).

[12] Lionel Trilling, "The Function of the Little Magazine," introduction to *The Partisan Reader: Ten Years of* Partisan Review, *1933–1944: An Anthology*, ed. William Phillips and Philip Rahv (New York: Dial Press, 1946).

[13] Christopher Lasch, "Ten Years of Salmagundi," *Salmagundi* no. 31/32 (Fall 1975–Winter 1976).

[14] Lionel Trilling, "The Function of the Little Magazine," introduction to *The Partisan Reader: Ten Years of* Partisan Review, *1933–1944: An Anthology*, ed. William Phillips and Philip Rahv (New York: Dial Press, 1946).

[15] Susan Sontag, "Remembering Barthes," *New York Review of Books*, May 15, 1980; reprinted in Susan Sontag, *Under the Sign of Saturn* (New York: Farrar, Straus and Giroux, 1980).

[16] Jean Amery, quoted in W. G. Sebald's *On the Natural History of Destruction* (New York: Random House, 2003).

[17] "Susan Sontag and Philip Fisher: A Conversation," *Salmagundi*, no. 139/140 (2003).

[18] Adam Phillips, *Attention Seeking* (London: Penguin 2019).

[19] George Steiner, "A Tale of Three Cities," in *George Steiner at the New Yorker* (New York: New Directions, 2009).

[20] Susan Sontag, "Notes on 'Camp,'" *Partisan Review* 31, no. 4 (1964); republished in Susan Sontag and David Rieff, *Essays of the 1960s & 70s: Against Interpretation; Styles of Radical Will; On Photography; Illness as Metaphor; Uncollected Essays* (New York: Library of America, 2013).

[21] Robert Boyers, "Steiner's Literary Journalism: 'The heart of the maze,'" in *Reading George Steiner*, ed. Nathan A. Scott Jr. and Ronald A. Sharp (Baltimore: Johns Hopkins University Press, 1994).

[22] Joseph Epstein, "Curious George," review of Steiner's *Lessons of the Masters*, *Washington Examiner*, February 16, 2004.

[23] George Steiner, "Text and Context," *Salmagundi*, no. 31/32 (Fall 1975–Winter 1976).

[24] Robert Boyers and William Deresiewicz, "The Death of the Artist: Excellent Sheep: An Interview with William Deresiewicz," *Salmagundi*, no. 210/211 (2021).

[25] Joseph Joubert, *The Notebooks of Joseph Joubert*, trans. Paul Auster (New York: New York Review Books Classics, 2005).

[26] Deborah Eisenberg, "Becoming Susan Sontag," *New York Review of Books*, December 18, 2008.

[27] Robert Boyers, "On Susan Sontag and the New Sensibility," *Salmagundi*, no. 3 (1966).

[28] Rick Moody, "Against Cool," in *On Celestial Music: And Other Adventures in Listening* (New York: Little Brown, 2012).

[29] Susan Sontag, *Against Interpretation and Other Essays* (New York: Farrar, Straus and Giroux, 1966).

[30] Adrienne Rich and Susan Sontag, "Feminism and Fascism: An Exchange," *New York Review of Books*, February 6, 1975.

[31] Susan Sontag, "The Third World of Women," *Partisan Review* 40, no. 2 (1973).

[32] Jack Kerouac, *The Dharma Bums* (New York: Penguin, 1976), quoted in Moody, "Against Cool."

[33] Elias Canetti, *The Torch in My Ear*, trans. Joachim Neugroschel (New York: Farrar, Straus and Giroux, 1982).

[34] Canetti, *Torch in My Ear*.

[35] Stendhal, *The Red and the Black* (New York: Norton, 1969).

[36] Philip Rieff, *The Triumph of the Therapeutic: Uses of Faith After Freud* (New York: Harper and Row, 1966).

[37] Clement Greenberg, "Avant-Garde and Kitsch," in *Art and Culture* (New York: Beacon Press, 1965).

[38] Transcript of Symposium On Kitsch, *Salmagundi* no. 85/86 (Winter 1990).

[39] Susan Sontag, at a rally in support of Poland's Solidarity Movement at the Town Hall on West 43rd Street, Manhattan, February 6, 1982.

[40] Lionel Trilling, "The Fate of Pleasure," in *Beyond Culture: Essays on Literature and Learning* (New York: Viking, 19965).

[41] Joan Acocella, quoted in Benjamin Moser, *Sontag: Her Life and Work* (New York: Ecco, 2019).

[42] Robert Coles, review of Philip Rieff, *The Triumph of the Therapeutic: Uses of Faith After Freud, New York Times Book Review*, February 6, 1966.

[43] Philip Rieff, *The Triumph of the Therapeutic: Uses of Faith After Freud* (New York: Harper and Row, 1966).

[44] Philip Rieff, *Fellow Teachers* (London: Faber & Faber, 1975).

[45] Susan Sontag, foreword to Robert Walser, *Selected Stories* (New York: New York Review Books Classics, 2002).

[46] Edmund Wilson, *The Bit Between My Teeth: A Literary Chronicle of 1950–1965* (New York: Farrar, Straus and Giroux, 1965).

[47] Susan Sontag, *Where the Stress Falls: Essays* (Farrar, Straus and Giroux, 2001).

[48] Susan Sontag, "The Ideal Husband," *New York Review of Books*, September 26, 1963.

[49] Susan Sontag, *At the Same Time: Essays and Speeches* (New York: Macmillan, 2007).

[50] Quoted in Benjamin Moser, *Susan Sontag: Her Life and Work* (New York: Ecco, 2019).

[51] Quoted in Moser, *Susan Sontag*.

[52] Robert Boyers, "Exploration and Conviction in Godard, *A Married Woman*" *Georgia Review* 30, no. 3 (Fall 1976).

[53] Janet Malcolm, "The Unholy Practice," review of Benjamin Moser, *Susan Sontag: Her Life and Work*, *New Yorker*, September 3, 2019.

[54] Robert Boyers, *Lionel Trilling: Negative Capability and the Wisdom of Avoidance* (Columbia, MO: University of Missouri Press, 1977).

[55] Leslie H. Farber, *The Ways of the Will: Essays Toward a Psychology and Psychopathology of Will* (New York: Basic Books, 1966).

[56] George Steiner, "The Archives of Eden," *Salmagundi*, no. 50/51 (1981).

[57] Susan Sontag, "What's Happening in America," *Partisan Review* (Winter 1967).

[58] George Steiner, *In Bluebeard's Castle: Some Notes Towards the Redefinition of Culture* (New Haven, CT: Yale University Press, 1971).

[59] Edward Said, review of *George Steiner: A Reader*, *Nation*, May 2, 1985.

[60] Edward W. Said, "Steiner's *Exterritorial: Papers on Literature and the Language Revolution*, *New York Times Book Review* (August 1, 1971).

[61] Irving Howe, "Auschwitz and High Mandarin," review of George Steiner, *In Bluebeard's Castle*, *Harper's Magazine*, July 1969.

[62] Irving Howe, *Salmagundi*, no. 85/86 (1990).

[63] These George Steiner lectures were published as *The Lessons of the Masters: The Charles Eliot Norton Lectures* (Cambridge, MA: Harvard University Press, 2003).

[64] Adam Gopnik, "The Seriousness of George Steiner," *New Yorker*, February 5, 2020.

[65] Salman Rushdie, *Step Across This Line: Collected Nonfiction 1992–2002* (New York: Random House, 2002).

[66] John Carroll, "George Steiner and Cambridge English: A Dismal Case of Rancour," *Meanjin Quarterly* 32, no. 3 (September 1973).

[67] George Steiner, "In Lieu of a Preface," *Salmagundi*, no. 58/59 (1982–1983).

[68] James O'Higgins and Michel Foucault, "Sexual Choice, Sexual Act: An Interview with Michel Foucault," *Salmagundi*, no. 58/59 (Fall 1982–Winter 1983).

[69] Jill Johnson, "Lesbian/Feminism Reconsidered," *Salmagundi*, no. 58/59 (Fall 1982–Winter 1983).

[70] Paul Robinson, "In the First Person: 'Dear Paul': An Exchange Between Teacher and Student," *Salmagundi*, no. 58/59 (Fall 1982–Winter 1983).

[71] Arno Karlen, "The New Lesbian Politics and the Decline of Social Science," *Salmagundi*, no. 58/59 (Fall 1982–Winter 1983).

[72] Robert Alter, "Proust and the Ideological Reader," *Salmagundi*, no. 58/59 (Fall 1982–Winter 1983).

[73] George Steiner, "Silence and the Poet," in *Language and Silence: Essays on Language, Literature, and the Inhuman* (New York: Atheneum, 1967).

[74] George Steiner, "Night Words: High Pornography and Human Privacy," in *Language and Silence*.

[75] George Steiner, "A Kind of Survivor," *Commentary* (February 1965).

[76] Terrence Des Pres, review of George Steiner, *Antigones, Nation*, March 2, 1985.

[77] Ronald A. Sharp and George Steiner, "George Steiner, The Art of Criticism, No. 2," interview with George Steiner, *Paris Review*, no. 137 (Winter, 1995).

[78] George Steiner, "Bad Friday," *New Yorker*, March 2, 1992; reprinted in *George Steiner at the New Yorker* (New York: New Directions, 2009).

[79] George Steiner, *George Steiner at the New Yorker* (New York: New Directions, 2009).

[80] James Wood, *The Broken Estate: Essays on Literature and Belief* (New York: Random House, 1999).

[81] George Steiner recommendation for "Best Book of the Year," *Times Literary Supplement*, December 2–8, 1988.

[82] Terrence Des Pres, review of George Steiner, *Antigones*, *Nation*, March 2, 1985.

[83] Terrence Des Pres, review of George Steiner, *Antigones*, *Nation*, March 2, 1985.

[84] James Wood, *The Broken Estate: Essays on Literature and Belief* (New York: Random House, 1999).

[85] Henry Hardy, *In Search of Isaiah Berlin: A Literary Adventure* (New York: Tauris Parke, 2020).

[86] Henry Hardy, letter to the editor, *Times Literary Supplement*, April 10, 2020.

[87] James Wood's essay "George Steiner's Unreal Presence" is reprinted in Wood's *The Broken Estate: Essays on Literature and Belief* (New York: Random House, 1999).

[88] Alfred Kazin, blurb for George Steiner, *No Passion Spent: Essays 1978–1995* (London: Faber & Faber, 1996).

[89] George Steiner, *Real Presences: Is There Anything in What We Say?* (London: Faber & Faber, 1989).

[90] Bernard Knox, review of *Antigones*, *New Republic*, 1984; reprinted in Bernard Knox, *Essays Ancient and Modern* (Baltimore, MD: Johns Hopkins University Press, 1989).

[91] Naomi Bliven, review of George Steiner, *After Babel*, *New Yorker*, May 5, 1975.

[92] Eric Hombery, George Steiner obituary in the *Guardian*, February 5, 2020.

[93] Adam Gopnik, "The Seriousness of George Steiner," *New Yorker*, February 5, 2020.

[94] Christopher Hitchens, *Letters to a Young Contrarian* (New York: Basic Books, 2005).

[95] Karl Kraus, *No Compromise: Selected Writings* of Karl Kraus (New York: Ungar, 1977).

[96] Roger Kimball, "Is the Future Just a Tense?" *New York Times Book Review*, September 2, 2001.

[97] George Steiner, *Language and Silence: Essays on Language, Literature and the Inhuman* (New York: Atheneum, 1967).

[98] George Steiner, *Language and Silence: Essays on Language, Literature and the Inhuman* (New York: Atheneum, 1967).

[99] Susan Sontag, *Under the Sign of Saturn* (New York: Macmillan, 1980).

[100] Susan Sontag, *Under the Sign of Saturn* (New York: Macmillan, 1980).

NAMES INDEX